D1046777

ON THE AGENDA OF DEMOCRACY

LONDON : HUMPHREY MILFORD

OXFORD UNIVERSITY PRESS

ON THE AGENDA OF DEMOCRACY

BY

CHARLES E. MERRIAM

Vice-Chairman of the National Resources Planning Board

CAMBRIDGE, MASSACHUSETTS
HARVARD UNIVERSITY PRESS
1941

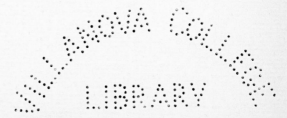

COPYRIGHT, 1941
BY THE PRESIDENT AND FELLOWS OF HARVARD COLLEGE

PRINTED AT THE HARVARD UNIVERSITY PRESS
CAMBRIDGE, MASSACHUSETTS, U.S.A.

C
123
14

EDWIN LAWRENCE GODKIN

1831–1902

EDWIN LAWRENCE GODKIN, editor of *The Nation* and the New York *Evening Post*, was born in Ireland of English stock, and took his degree at Queen's College, Belfast, in 1851. He published a *History of Hungary* and was associated with the London *Daily News* and the Belfast *Northern Whig* before coming to America in 1856. Here his letters to the *Daily News* on American public affairs attracted attention and prepared him for the task he assumed in 1865 as first editor of *The Nation*, to which he gave a scholarly quality, a breadth of view, and a moral tone that brought it recognition as one of the best weeklies in the English-speaking world. In 1881 *The Nation* became the weekly edition of the New York *Evening Post*, of which Godkin was made editor in chief in 1883. From that time until his retirement in 1900 he exercised an influence on public opinion out of all proportion to the circulation of his paper. Editors throughout the country, whether in sympathy with his views or not, watched for his editorials on all important issues. He was exceptionally well read in economics, history, and political theory, believed wholeheartedly in democracy, owed allegiance to no person or party, and was vigorous and fearless in expression. In 1903, by a gift to Harvard University, his friends established "The Godkin Lectures on the Essentials of Free Government and the Duties of the Citizen" in appreciation of his long and disinterested service to the country of his adoption and in the hope of stimulating that spirit of independent thought and devotion to the public service which characterized his career.

52162

Preface

A WORD regarding my own relations with Mr. Godkin may not be amiss by way of introduction. During the years when I was a student in the Columbia University School of Political Science, I was a reader of the New York *Evening Post*, a recruit in the battles against Tammany, and an interested reader of Mr. Godkin's *Problems of Modern Democracy* in 1896, and his *Unforeseen Tendencies of Democracy* in 1898. The latter work, *Unforeseen Tendencies*, was a very challenging volume to me, for the writer raised questions not formulated earlier either by the friends or the foes of Democracy; — questions arising not so much from a philosophy of politics as from practical experience.

The *Unforeseen Tendencies* were summed up by Godkin under several heads. The first is the failure to vote. It was assumed by all those who advocated universal suffrage and by those who opposed it that men who got the ballot would use it. Godkin pointed out one of the Unforeseen Tendencies toward non-voting not anticipated by either the friends or opponents of democratic government. This is a topic I analyzed later in a volume entitled *Non-Voting* (with H. F. Gosnell, 1923).

The second Unforeseen Tendency is the representation of special interests rather than the general interest. Without argument it had been admitted by the opponents of democracy that when the mass of the people had the right to vote, the general interest would always be represented. It never occurred to critics that the represented interests would be special or private interests, nor did it occur to the friends of democracy that the representation might not be that of a general interest. In other words, it was never carefully considered what it was that would be represented in the struggle after the adoption of general suffrage.

Special interests, Godkin points out, are often able to control elections not only of representatives in the legislative sense, but in a more generalized sense. They may control by corrupt means large masses of voters. But here is something that never was considered, even by the opponents of democracy, — that when men got the vote, they would not vote in their own interest — that they would be twisted, turned and pulled over into the control of a piratical crew like that headed by Tweed or the Philadelphia gang. Not having foreseen these problems, we are now faced by them, and the question arises, what is the way out? Mr. Godkin did not profess to have the answer to all these problems, but he studied the situation.

Many new and also unforeseen problems have

sprung up in the years since 1898. In these lectures *On the Agenda of Democracy*, I propose
to outline the elements of a democratic program,
in the light of the generation of social and economic
development since Mr. Godkin wrote his essays.
Thus I hope to repay in part my debt to this striking figure of the '90's, through the medium of the
Godkin Lectures.

C. E. M.

University of Chicago
July 1, 1941

CONTENTS

Introduction

FOREMOST on the agenda of democracy is the reconsideration of the program in the light of modern conditions. The old world is gone and will not return. We face a new era, which searches all creeds, all forms, all programs of action, and spares none. Reason and science have made basic changes that demand readjustment at many points. Of all forms of political association democracy is fortunately the most flexible and the most easily adaptable to new conditions, for democracy has no need to protect any special interests of class or caste. Democracy does not forget the past, but it looks forward to a creative future. One of the chief tasks confronting democracy is the development of a program adequate to meet the changes of our time.

A preliminary to the program of democracy is a reconsideration of the theory of popular government, an analysis of the intellectual foundations of democratic political association. This is a task which I have essayed elsewhere,[1] however, and I shall not attempt it here.

[1] *The New Democracy and the New Despotism* (McGraw-Hill Book Co., 1939); *Prologue to Politics* (University of Chicago Press, 1939); *The Role of Politics in Social Change* (New York University Press, 1934); *What is Democracy?* (University of Chicago Press, 1941).

These lectures will deal with two parts of the democratic program:

I. The structural forms and general understandings adapted to modern democracy, or what I have described as streamlining democracy's organization.

II. New programs necessary to develop the democratic system adequately in our times, or restating the democratic bill of rights.

Under Part I come democracy and law-making, democracy and public administration, democracy and world order. Under Part II come democratic planning of our national resources, and democracy's new guarantees of the pursuit of happiness.

If anyone says that our main task at the present moment is that of effective national defense, I agree with him heartily. But I point out that an essential part of well-organized defense is a clear understanding of the democratic program. Democracy is not merely something to be defended and preserved, as it must and shall be through our united efforts, but an ideal to be developed and enriched, a constant approximation to higher standards of living and higher levels of the good life. The program discussed in these lectures is an outline of a part of the democratic program, as it emerges out of our troubled times.

PART I
STREAMLINING DEMOCRACY'S STRUCTURE

CHAPTER I

Democracy and Law-Making

ONE of the first items on the program of democracy is the streamlining of democratic machinery of government to meet the requirements of our times. The problem of streamlining democracy is not, as is too commonly supposed, a question closely related to the quantum of government or to its complexity. The fundamental problem is that of proportioning and organization. From the organizational point of view it is no more difficult to organize a nation of one hundred million than a nation of five million. The problems that perplex the tiniest states are not different in type from those of France or Spain or America. The categories are the same. For centuries it was assumed as a matter of course that a democracy must contain only a small number, say 10,000 — the number who could hear the voice of the orator in an assembly of the folk. Three million seemed difficult in the early days of the United States, but we learned not to be disturbed about 30 million or 60 or 100 or 120, and now we are worried perhaps because we are not to have more than 155 million at the top point. Instead of saying, "What shall we do with a million more every year?" we hear it said, "Well, what shall we do without any additional increments of population?"

Or whether the government does one hundred things or a thousand is not of primary significance, if these are the types of things that government in a particular moment of cultural evolution can undertake. A state may, of course, undertake activities which it should not try to carry through at a given time, and states have blundered at this point. A state might perhaps manage bonuses for increase of population, but would find it difficult to require a license for births as a means of restriction. Even the Russian government at the height of its power found difficulty in preventing handshaking and in requiring the turn to the right on sidewalks; and when it came to discouraging kissing, the all-powerful ones were routed — properly, I would say on behalf of the future. The totalitarian state soon comes upon the "poverty of power."

If we recede from the theory that government is a necessary evil and advance to the doctrine that government is a positive good, the problem of organization is far simpler. I recognize, however, that such a view is not easy for all people to take.

Much confusion has been caused by the unnecessary admission on the part of some of the friends of democracy that popular government is naturally and normally "inefficient," while autocratic governments are naturally and normally "efficient." Democratic political societies, it is said, may bring freedom but not efficiency. The truth is that there is nothing in our experience with management either to support the assertion or warrant the admission. Freedom and efficiency are not opposites, but complementary one to the other.

This new argument against freedom is only the old defense of slavery dressed up in new form. Turn it which way you will, said Lincoln, it is "the same old serpent." It is now three and a half centuries since Bodin denounced slavery, and countless proofs have been added until the contention that slave labor is more effective than free labor no longer is seriously and responsibly advanced. On the contrary, the superior productivity of free labor is everywhere put forth as elementary. Slavery has been abandoned long since and it will not be restored.

But in the field of government, curiously enough, the old and outworn tradition still lingers in the phrase that free governments are not and cannot be effective or efficient. It is even added that if democratic governments are effective it is because they are to that extent undemocratic. The proofs of this conclusion are not forthcoming and cannot be produced by the most diligent search. That democratic governments sometimes delay and sometimes are confused in counsels is true, but the same conditions prevail from time to time in despotic governments also. The czar of all the Russias or a Bourbon emperor endowed with all the juristic authority that lawyers could devise may fumble and be futile as well as any group in a democratic state. Concentration of authority does not necessarily carry with it capacity to use power effectively.[1]

Nor does power rest upon speed of decision determined by an individual judgment alone. There are always individuals and groups to be consulted in any human system of authority in times past and now. The difficulties at Munich were not due to a lack of power on the part of Chamberlain or of Daladier, but to a lack of ability to use effectively, in that particular situation, the authority they had. Mussolini a little later also demonstrated capacity for muddling. When the social tension is great enough, democratic agencies can decide with great speed, if necessary, but if there is no great social tension it is difficult for any ruler to inaugurate a sweeping policy profoundly affecting the ways of life among the people of the nation. The disparagement of the efficiency of the free state is only a survival of the earlier times when the mass was called the "mob," the "ignorant crowd," the "ignorant many" who were incapable of anything except assent to the mandates of their betters.

[1] See my *Political Power* (1934).

In the field of government the ranks of public administration were long recruited largely from the aristocracy, trained for that purpose, to the exclusion of the mass of the people. The development of modern scientific management and administrative management has upset this old and limited view of the possibilities of mankind. Universal education, universal opportunity for administrative service, modern discoveries regarding the meaning of morale, development of leadership in labor — all these factors have changed our ideas of the relation of democracy to efficiency in industry, in administration, and even in the armies of the world. Purely arbitrary, raw personal will as a basis of authority tends to disappear in modern society, whatever may seem to rise on the surface for the moment. Coöperation, fraternity, rational principles of guidance, scientific management of administration come into the workings of modern organization, whether political or industrial. The democratic system instead of being inefficient is, just the contrary, in line with the highest standards of efficiency now being established. Freedom brings efficiency more fully and effectively than slavery. No one even considers a slave organization of factories, mines, and farms in these days.

What to some seems like efficiency on the part of non-democratic governments arises from a confusion of the ends and the means of government.

If a state wills war and conquest and prepares over a long period for war and conquest while other states prepare for peace, the resulting conflict does not indicate the relative abilities of the respective states with differing ideas. War preparation by one non-democratic state would have made its war administration seem superior to that of another non-democratic state without warlike aims. Germany and Italy are non-democratic states, but their results measured in terms of efficiency were not the same. The British navy developed by a democratic state on the other hand was definitely superior to the Italian navy developed under Fascism. The United States could have developed a vast apparatus of planes, tanks, and armored divisions, had it willed to lend its national energies to war and conquest. The Soviets willed to set up a demonstration of a particular economic theory, and to accomplish this through a form of dictatorship. The government assumed the broadest legal powers, but this did not automatically ensure it against governmental and economic inefficiency.

There is nothing in the categories of organization to indicate that a democratic society cannot set up forms of authority adequate to all social situations, normal or critical, providing for the determination of policy by a council and for administrative management under the general control and supervision of the determiners of policy. The successful operation of any system, such as the American or the British, rests upon a resolute will to set up a free political system, and the political sophistication necessary to sustain it in practice. That great armies, great governmental projects, great quasi-public and private industries can be set up and that high standards of living can be progressively developed under such free institutions is beyond all doubt.

It is necessary to reconsider democracy at this point, and discover not only where we stand but where we are going. In war times, we are agreed that everything must be done that is necessary for the winning of the war. But about peace-time objectives we are not so sure or so resolute, although the ends of public welfare may be equally important and even urgent. Some day it will dawn upon us that all the clauses in the Preamble to the Constitution are worth fighting for.

The problem of streamlining democracy must deal with the broad subject of the organization of the policy-determining agencies, and with the organization of executive leadership and of administrative management; and this in the light of modern conditions. Some of the changes required will be formal and others will be informal; some will call for changes in laws and mechanisms; others will be brought about by general understandings which lie at the root of any political society and which are

especially significant in a democratic state. Fortunately our Constitution is broad enough in its terms,
flexible enough in its spirit, and capable of liberal
enough interpretation by the judiciary to permit
the adaptation of democracy to changing conditions without serious difficulty. And fortunately
the temper of our American people is such as to
look with favor upon necessary changes in industry and government alike, when practical necessity
or advantage is before them.

For a wide variety of reasons — sometimes conflicting reasons, indeed — the policy-determining
agencies have been under severe fire from many
quarters, both right and left. Legislative bodies are
incompetent, it may be said, or corrupt, or dilatory,
or unrepresentative of the general interest of the
community, or falling short of the omni-compe-
tence that would be required of a successful legis-
lator in our complicated times. The elective process
is not favorable to the choice of the leaders of the
community, and mediocrity takes their place, it is
alleged. Legislatures are given to debate and delay,
to inconclusiveness and lack of dynamic drive. The
conclusion has been drawn by Hitler and others
that the way out is the abolition of legislative bodies
or their reduction to purely ceremonial bodies
assembling to ratify, but not to deliberate upon or
to reject, proposals submitted to them.

It is necessary to recur to basic factors in this

whole policy-determining process before drawing conclusions.[1] First we must recall that the whole legislative process is relatively new in the history of mankind. Customs, decrees, interpretations, codifications, and some few laws — these were the commonplace of early political direction. Mass making of mass rules thus brings with it a double problem: one, that of legislation itself; and the other, that of common determination of the basic policies affecting the common good. More laws have been made in the past century than in all the history of politics. And the United States, counting the forty-eight states and the Nation, makes as many laws as all the rest of the world.

The present effort to discredit democratic representation rests upon the despot's policies of (1) personal assumption of responsibility for the common weal, without any accountability; and (2) direct appeal to the mass through the agencies of the radio, and organization of mass symbolism and propaganda over the heads of parties, parliaments, and sundry social groupings — all assimilated to the main purpose and directive, and supplemented by violence. The first of these is as old as despotism in its various forms, running back hundreds of years. The second only is new — the product of technical discoveries in intercommunication.

A student of political behavior cannot predict the

[1] T. V. Smith, *The Legislative Way of Life* (1940).

outcome of military struggles such as that in which the world is now engaged, but he can observe the growing importance of the role of representation in industry, in government, in scientific management of industrial enterprise, as well as in political management, even in the military establishments. He sees the basis for consent in the rising standards of education and intelligence, and in equal access to minimum security and participation in the gains of civilization. Whatever may happen in moments of tension and convulsion, he sees the ultimate return to institutions through which the deepest sources of power, morale, and happiness are reached.

It is important to assay the role of legislative bodies in general to find a basis of appraisal. The primary role of a legislative assembly is that of unifying the wisdom and the will of the community. It is on the one hand an instrument for utilizing the social intelligence of the community, and on the other, of formulating and expressing the will of the community. This will in turn rests upon special interests and general interests in some form of balance. The legislative body is the symbol of this fusion of reason and will, presumably reached after discussion and debate dealing with all the significant aspects of the given decision.

The general temper of the representative organization is more important than its structure. The process of wisely formulating broad measures ex-

pressing the common judgment on the common-
weal is not a matter of technical procedure primarily,
or even of fine draftsmanship, however important
the latter may be. The legislative process is that of
translating a popular decision into a general directive — a process of turning the wisdom and the will
of the state into broad lines of administrative action,
and this on the basis of responsibility and accountability. The overshadowing, over-all problem is
the determination of what is the common good and
the formulation of it in adequate policies. In the
determination of what is the common good there
inevitably figures a balance of interests of multiple
sorts as diverse as the variety of social interests in
the state. These interests may be implemented by
the social intelligence of the community in the form
of broad mandates of community action. The
requisite quality of lawmakers is not primarily the
highest technical competence, but insight, wisdom,
prudence, judgment, social diplomacy, and the
ability to bring a confusion of voices into something like a central harmony, commanding the support of the bulk of the community.

It is idle to say smartly that nothing is accomplished through "talk," through legislative deliberation and discussion. "Talk" is a phase of decision
in many walks of life outside the political; and
within the political field talk is not confined to the
legislative halls of democratic states. The govern-

ments of Germany and Italy are not mere dumb shows. The legislative halls may be closed, but debate goes on none the less in invisible parliaments, in boudoirs, in banquet halls, in *chambres introuvables*, where argument is long and loud, although not fully known or reported by the press. What did Hitler say to Mussolini; or Stalin to Ribbentrop? And when great decisions are made, does the line of action emerge automatically from the vasty deep, or was there discussion and division before there was decision?

Historical memoirs authenticated years afterward show us clearly the lines of talk which characterized the despotic states of the world over long ranges of time. The despot may decide in the last instance, but if he is wise he will listen to the debates before he closes his mind upon a line of policy.

The practical question is how well is the argument set up to develop points of view, to lead to the truth; how well organized is the occasion for that form of interchange of ideas and interests upon which any government must rely, democratic or otherwise?

Reorganization of representative systems has always been one of the critical interests of students of government and democracy, and is now. The various devices contrived have been numerous and sometimes ingenious, but none yet developed is fundamental. They are important, but not fundamentally important, since they deal with details rather than with the larger principles really involved. Whether a representative body should contain two houses or one or three, whether one house should be an industrial parliament, whether the system of elections should be based on proportional representation or on the present plan, whether geographic areas should be the units of representation or whether some occupational underpinning should be provided — all these are proper matters of discussion by technicians, but they do not lead to anything decisive in dealing with the broad problem of democratic association. Even the problem of parliamentary versus presidential government does not reach down to the roots of the question. It is quite possible to set up a democratic state and operate it successfully under either of these systems, as the English and the American experience demonstrate.

I do not contend that the methods of selecting and the forms of composition of legislative bodies might not be materially improved, but I do not find any great promise in the methods proposed, or any great help in the basic problem of streamlining our democratic system to meet the needs of modern times.

From my point of view, in the American scene a much more effective device than any of these complicated systems would be startlingly simple.

As in olden times the mandate "Go wash in Jordan seven times" was rejected because it seemed too easy and too inadequate, so my recommendation may likewise be summarily dismissed. I should recommend the lowly device of doubling the salaries of all Congressmen, so that they may have $20,000 a year instead of $10,000 a year. And I will even go farther and allow them a form of civil pension after a number of years' service. This would cost us a half-million dollars a year, but that is not a heavy charge on our present-day budget. We are now endeavoring to recruit the finest type of legislative personnel on a basis that calls for too great a sacrifice on the part of the representatives. Ten thousand a year may seem large in some areas, but if the expenses of nomination are deducted and the expenses of the election are deducted and the expense of maintaining a hostel in Washington for the benefit of constituents is deducted, and if the loss and cost of ten of the best years of the representative's life are deducted, it will be found that the average Congressman is making a considerable personal contribution to the maintenance and operation of the legislative mill.

In many of our states the legislative compensation is absurdly inadequate. Kansas, Michigan, and Oregon pay legislators $3 per day, with the stipulation in Kansas that compensation is not to exceed $150 for regular, or $90 for special, sessions. In

Alabama, Tennessee, and Utah the rate is $4 per day. Connecticut's legislators receive $300 for two years. In New Hampshire they are paid $200 per term, and in Vermont $400 for two years. Eight other states reward legislators at the rate of $5 per day. Massachusetts, however, is much more appreciative of the efforts of its lawmakers and gives them $2000 per session.[1]

The legislative functions are often misunderstood. They are not problems of detail but of broad principle. These functions include the following:

1. Fiscal allocations of national resources for the general good.
2. Formulation of basic decisions and broad directives of national policy.
3. General supervision of administration and development of ways and means of securing the accountability of administration through legislation.
4. The organization of democratic controversy on a high level, where divergence of principles and policy may be clearly stated for effective national consideration.

Streamlining our legislative democracy is not primarily a matter of new laws but of new under-

[1] *The Book of the States, 1939–40*, vol. III (Council of State Governments, Chicago, 1939), p. 56.

standings and practices. I do not undertake to set up a comprehensive arrangement of new devices, but content myself with a few indications of general directions.[1]

For illustration, the significance of a unified budget in the making of fiscal allowances is very great. There are now in round numbers some fifteen budgets alongside a series of miscellaneous appropriation bills. These might be brought together so that the whole fiscal policy of the United States might be considered as one significant measure of far-reaching importance. In this connection the item veto might be conferred upon the President of the United States either by the long way of Constitutional amendment, or by the short way of house rules which might be adopted. All this would not diminish the real authority and dignity of the Congress, but by shifting the emphasis from detail to general principles would amplify and enlarge its position in the American democracy.

In such a broad discussion the relation of national expenditures to national income would inevitably be raised, and the appropriation bill become one of the central points in national policy along with

[1] I may say in passing that a careful scrutiny of the role and processes of legislative activity in the United States would have very great value if competently carried out by the Congress itself. Such an inquiry might well have been a coördinate of the 1935–37 inquiry on administrative management. It would be interesting to note what veterans like Senator Norris of Nebraska might say regarding the ideal organization and process of Congress.

considerations of long-time planning. Emphasis would be shifted from considerations of detail to questions of broad national policy upon which the representative body with its breadth of view would be able to present very important considerations, more effectively than in the treatment of details in piecemeal fashion.

The formulation of broad policies on a sounder basis would involve (1) the better equipment of Congress with technical information and perhaps the ampler use of information now on hand, and (2) change in emphasis from detail in legislation to broad statement of general directives. There are, to be sure, times when a detail is inextricably inter-woven with a principle, but in general this is not true. The abiding strength of Congress is not in dotting *i*'s and crossing *t*'s, but in lucid statement of guiding lines of national direction.

It is possible to maintain effective control over broad national policy through a relatively small number of directing statutes, broad in nature but pointed in direction and general purpose. The strength of the Constitution was its brevity and its generality in combination. A constitution ten times as long and detailed would have been far less effective in its impact upon national policy. The tendency of legislative bodies toward devotion to minute detail is not a sign of strength but of weakness, and continued elaboration of language indicates a drift toward inadequacy of general supervisory power, which may now be considered.

A most significant field of legislative activity is the adequate general supervision of administration. Some of the most effective work of Congress has been accomplished by special inquiries, breaking through impenetrable jungles of bureaucracy or vested privilege, or by routine inquiries or investigations. It has been suggested that a sound procedure would be the organization of joint committees of House and Senate dealing with the important problems of personnel, of budget, and of planning — these from the over-all point of view. Obviously the rivalry of legislative bodies makes this difficult to organize or to operate, but from the point of view of the democracy as a whole, which the legislative body represents, an opportunity would be afforded for the focusing of public attention upon a broad review of administrative activities — not primarily in detail but in principle. If these inquiries are punitive in purpose or method the results will be less satisfactory, but there is room for broad and fruitful investigations of the very greatest value to the state.

To what extent a representative body really serves as the center of controversy in the national state is itself a subject of excited discussion. Herr Hitler evidently lost his way when he first looked down upon what he called the antics of the Austrian parliament. Many others since then have lost the way. In streamlining representation and legislation we are met by the challenge of a revolution in modes of intercommunication. What is the bearing of the press, the radio, the cinema upon modern interchange of ideas and emotions? In this complex world, what is the impact of intercommunication upon the representative body, and how shall it shape its behavior to meet the new demands upon it? In some august assemblies, it is true, the device of electrical voting has been introduced. Shall we broadcast the proceedings of Congress? And if so, what influence would this have upon the tone and tenor of Congressional debate? Would it rise or fall? Would this tend to democratic illumination and edification, or would the opposite ensue? What would be the deliberations of the ideal legislature if we were to let loose our imaginations and project our invention on a somewhat Utopian basis?

I do not know the answer to all this, but I know that the answer must be sought and found. The answer will not be discovered merely in the form of a rule, a regulation, or a law, but in an understanding regarding the role of law-making bodies in a democratic association. One may express the judgment that the solution will be found somewhere around the raising of the level of discussion, with broader principles and sharper definition of underlying issues. This is not the work of a legislative body alone. It can only be the result of an effective demand on the part of an enlightened community. In the long run, representatives represent what there is to be represented — not much more and not much less — not as much less as many like to say. If we do not like the picture we see in the mirror we hold up, it nevertheless is ourselves. "The fault, dear Brutus, is not in our stars but in ourselves." In the ensuing discussion on the role of administrative management in a democracy it will be possible to indicate more clearly some specific aids to intelligent and representative legislation.

In America the importance of organizing intelligent discussion of broad public policies is greater than in more centralized states because no one government has full power. Effective action involves the coöperation of forty-nine governments in many cases, as well as cities and other local authorities. It is consequently important to reach a consensus widespread throughout the land, and resting upon a very broad basis of understanding. Under our constitutional system both states and the United States must agree upon many measures of social significance, as, for example, health, schools, housing, land use, water use, taxation. The foundation of such agreements may be laid in an interchange of views, a clearing of interests, a reconciliation of purposes, which a national debate may well set forth and develop. Modern methods of intercom-

munication present alternative procedures for discussion, but the dramatic character of a Congressional debate has not yet been superseded by
forums or by polls of whatever kind and value.

The important point in all this is, first, the recognition of the values of public discussion resting on
the basis of adequate data and analysis, and, second,
the disposition to find a solution through peaceful
consent rather than through division and violence.
From time to time the action of legislative bodies is
criticized because it is influenced by pressure groups
of one sort and another — agricultural, labor, industrial, and social. This view, however, reflects a
naïve conception of the political process among
mankind. What type of human association is it in
which there are no pressures and counterpressures
for group action of one type and another? It is
indeed these very pressures of individuals and interests that call for the balancing function of the
state. If all interests and pressures settled themselves
automatically, there would be no need for government at all. The stars would move in their courses
without any central control.

The appearance of these social and economic
interests is an inevitable phenomenon of social organization and control. In any form of government, whether that of the Many, the Few, or the
One, these or like pressures will exist and will be
reflected in one form or another. The interests may

be less obvious and less public, but their activity will be observed by anyone familiar with the operations of the governing process.

Behind the formal social legislation in a democracy there is a large body of non-political representative bodies of many types operating as a part of the democratic process. These groups are not repressed, intimidated, or controlled by the state, but their activity is encouraged in the interest of sound formulation of public policy — in the interest of the process of common consent to the broad policies of the nation. Some of these groups are able from time to time to dictate to the government their programs, but on the whole one is likely to be balanced by others, and the net contribution is that of a broader discussion of legislative policies.

Nothing is clearer from the study of human political behavior than the recurrence and persistence of the deliberative council in all forms of society under all manner of conditions. If one is thrown out, another comes in. Councils may become weak, decorative, submissive, and sycophantic, but this condition cannot be reckoned with permanently; and they rise again to power in another corner and in another garb. The despot himself will call a council into being, if there is not one at hand; his own council he will call it, and such it may be, for a while. He may in turn become the tool of his own council, slowly rising to power. The history of the

British parliament and of the American colonial governors is among the most striking and enlightening pictures in the gallery of politics.

The attempt of the democratic political association to bring such a council into intimate relationship with the community itself in consideration of the common good is one of the boldest and the most difficult attempted. This experiment presupposes that the political community is capable of choosing for its representatives men of competence, character, loyalty to the community, to provide an instrument of popular control. Many exceptions and failures may readily be noted, but no other and better method has yet been devised by the mind of man to bring about representation or rapport with the day-by-day authorities. With all of its imperfections no better way has been found or is in sight. The alternative is a council appointed by an irresponsible ruler to advise his irresponsibility.

CHAPTER II

Democracy and Public Administration

STREAMLINING the executive side of democracy is likewise a task of prime importance. What is on the agenda here? Three points are of great significance:

    I. The abolition of the spoils system.

    II. The position of the executive in the system of government.

    III. The development of administrative management.

I

The same democracy that gave us Jefferson as a champion of the people gave us an opponent of strong nationalism. The same democracy that gave us Andrew Jackson to overthrow the old aristocracy gave us the spoils system — rotation in office not at the point of political control but at the point of management of predetermined policies.

For over a half-century we have struggled to throw off the yoke of the patronage system. This battle has been won in principle, but not in detail.

The career service is on its way to decisive victory. The old-fashioned spoils system is on its way to the political museum. No tears will be shed at its funeral, nor will there be colorful celebrations of its anniversary. A long series of events and a powerful combination of forces, among them labor and women, have brought this about. I venture to say that the report of the Commission on Public Service Personnel and President Roosevelt's Committee on Administrative Management were important factors in this development.

The far-reaching influence of this change upon the type of political leadership and the nature of party and political life is scarcely yet realized in America. It is far simpler to sneer at all politics as insincere and dirty.

There is still a long way to go, however, even though there is general agreement on the broad principle. There are thirty-one states with a population of 58,000,000, and there are 1114 cities and 2880 counties with a population of 31,000,000, without merit systems. Furthermore, in many jurisdictions the merit law is by no means effectively enforced, or perhaps is clumsily and ineffectively carried out. There remains an important job of ensuring the genuine application of the merit principle to the public service.

II

The more adequate organization of executive authority in the United States is on the agenda. From the establishment of the Constitution, provision was made — as a result of sad experience under the Articles of Confederation — for an executive of significance. In cities and states this example was followed only very slowly. In the '90's came what was called the municipal dictator or strong-mayor plan, as in New York City. In the states the executive powers were slowly gathered together, and in more recent years the organization of something in the nature of a cabinet form of state government has sprung up at various points.

In the meantime powerful executives appeared in industry and in labor. Later the critical world situation emphasized the importance of effective leadership in democratic states. Paradoxically, the very fear of dictators, so called, was turned into an argument against protective forms by which alone the domination by dictators may be prevented from extending over America.

Many notable volumes have recently been written on the executive, and it is not my intention to compete with them — with Herring, with Corwin, with Laski.[1] I shall content myself with the discus-

[1] Edward Pendleton Herring, *Presidential Leadership* (1940); Edward S. Corwin, *The President, Office and Powers* (1940);

sion of a few of the outstanding problems of over-whelming concern.

First of all, what new knowledge have we students of government regarding the nature and powers of the executive — knowledge that might usefully be applied to the present-day problems of statecraft?

In recent years we have acquired deeper insights into the nature of political leadership and the organization of the consent of the governed. From these types of analysis we may obtain additional material of significance in the organization of executive authority. From studies of leadership and of the milieu in which leadership operates we may derive directives regarding the problem of the executive in modern democracy.

Capacity for initiative and for sustained action, relations to technicians, contacts with the policy-determining agencies, facility in management, and forms of effective accountability — all these loom large in the emerging picture of the ideal executive. Institutional contrivances and understandings facilitating the exercise of these powers are of great importance and have been deeply studied in recent times.

Out of the mist of many analyses from diverse sources comes clearer understanding of the quali-

---

Harold J. Laski, *The American Presidency, an Interpretation* (1940).

ties of leaders. First of all come the qualities of non-leaders, now better and more widely understood, and then the more positive and difficult qualities of leaders. We now know that leadership is a more widely distributed capacity than was earlier supposed; indeed, we know that leadership would be impossible unless there were a supporting body of potential leaders to appreciate what was proposed or done. We know more about training for leadership, and training for appreciation of qualities of leadership. We know that the world is full of unrecognized leaders who rise when the regular leaders disappear, to the surprise and sometimes indeed the dismay of those who thought that wisdom would perish with them. This is evident in revolutionary movements, in social upturns of all types, in great crises when emergency action must be taken without the aid of the leaders by status. Recently in London, for example, "little people" were constantly springing up to lead — much to the chagrin perhaps of their social superiors, but to the satisfaction of those who were served.

The modern world is filled with leaders who came from nowhere. What powers may or should be entrusted to leaders, and what the rules, regulations, conventions, and understandings should be in a democratic society is a problem for which a high level of sophistication and discrimination is required. The European solution seen in Naziism and Fascism is not an answer at all, but an avoidance or postponement of the answer. Despotism is no advance over the centuries of ancient tyranny. Not even enlightened despotism is the answer in these days of awakened mankind. Leaders who choose themselves and are accountable only to themselves are not the answer to the continuing problem of the organization of political society, but a declaration of bankruptcy. Even if they are successful for the time, the broad problem is still to be considered and determined.

On the other hand, peoples democratic or otherwise who cannot adjust their institutions and choices to the needs of emergency decision are likewise doomed — for the opposite reason. If they cannot trust themselves to use the powers of their community for the common good — nay, the common life — they will not survive. Fear, distrust, suspicion — these are not the bases of vital power. States are not strong in proportion as their government is weak. Liberty is not secure in proportion as government has no power. Protection at home and abroad is the life of liberty — protection against special groups at home and against warlike powers abroad. Wars cannot be conducted without wide-ranging authority in the hands of the leader; and important social changes cannot be made without wide powers of policy and administration in the hands of the leaders. Not to trust any leaders is not to trust yourself — the formula for weakness and dissolution. Graveyards are full of timid men and timid nations who died because they trusted no one.

Demagogues and despots are alike the foes of the common weal. But between them is the possibility of democratic leaders, democratically chosen and democratically responsible to the community they serve.

III

From the new science and art of administrative management, democratically based, we derive in modern times much support for the institution of leadership. Here are provided the technical tools by which (a) various proposals may be technically checked; (b) proposals may be initiated; (c) policies may be applied and developed to meet social situations.

In earlier times administrators were recruited from the ruling class in large measure, and hence tended to apply and perpetuate the view and the interests of the ruling group, whether that group was despotic in form or aristocratic. This was true in Germany, in Austria, in France, even in England until recent times. Extraordinary capacity might of course break through and up, but in the main the recruits came from the dominant classes.

In a democratic society all the rich resources of the mass development of talent are available for the service of the state, as well as for any other enterprise. Their administration is no longer class management in the spirit and in the interest of a class, but mass management from the point of view of the mass and in the common interest. Their common good is not merely emotion, envy, misunderstanding, greed, but intelligence springing from technical knowledge and competence. This is a transformation of a revolutionary nature, more revolutionary than most revolutions, yet attracting relatively little attention since it is not accompanied by blood and thunder.

As an outgrowth of the report of the President's Committee on Administrative Management (1937) three outstanding results were obtained. One was the reorganization of departments and agencies. Three new agencies were created — the Federal Security, the Federal Works, and the Federal Loan. Under these and the original departments a redistribution of many federal authorities was made, although many exceptions were provided by law. Another was the adoption of the merit system and the career system in its broadest form. The third was the setting up of the Executive Office of the President in September 1939. Together they constitute a significant reorganization of the authority of the Executive, and are the technical basis for over-all information and analysis.[1]

The program of democracy calls for a sounder understanding of the relations between the executive and the legislative authority. Otherwise the ship of state may be wrecked upon this rock.

All this involves not so much a change in law or rule as a change in the general understanding of the relations of President and Congress. It does not involve the subordination of President to Congress as in the parliamentary system, nor the opposite, subordination of Congress to the Executive. Neither does it require, as some have suggested, the presence of the executive on the floor of the legislative body for purposes of adequate debate and discussion. What is involved is broader discussion in broader terms of national policy, less of detail and more of broad consideration. Executive authority belongs with the executive, while powers of appropriation, of general policy determination, of over-all inspection and supervision are within the hands of the legislature. They might be more effectively exercised to provide a more effective position of the legislature in the commonwealth.

A discussion of a unified budget, presented to Congress by the executive, would afford opportunity for a broad statement of competing principles regarding the entire fiscal policy of the

[1] *Public Administration Review*, vol. I, no. 2, March 1941.

government in its many wide ramifications into
economic policy. A discussion of the reports of
joint committees on personnel, on planning, and
on fiscal policy and management would afford opportunity for general consideration of the total
situation at any given time in the affairs of state.
An appropriating and supervising body has many
ways of expressing its assent or approval of administrative action, and should be fully equipped to do
so, with technical material and room for deliberation.

These words, I realize, can readily be twisted
into a charge that an attempt is being made to re-
strict, restrain, crib, cabin, and confine the legislative body in the interest of the executive. I pause
therefore to say with all possible emphasis that this
is a suggestion for broadening and strengthening
the powers of the legislative body, and making it
an even more important factor in national organization. Legislative bodies are not strong in detail
but in general principle; they are most competent,
not in the minutiae of government, but in the determination of the general directives of governmental action. The very greatest quality of the
Constitution in the opinion of many notable com-
mentators is the broad sweep of its language, its
success in enunciating general principles of political
action. As state constitutions grew longer and
longer they became weaker and weaker, and as

state and national statutes became longer and longer they lost some of their original values.

It is the reaction from this practice that has led to the organization of administrative agencies with wide discretionary powers in recent times — with what are termed sub-legislative powers. Long accepted in most democratic states, these powers were within the last generation set up in the United States, and have operated with notable success. In recent years the number of non-Cabinet agencies has greatly increased. This dispersion of executive authority through a long and increasing series of independent regulatory agencies operated adversely, as was pointed out by the President's Committee.

The Committee was not interested in the number of departments or forms of government, but in the working organization of whatever departments, agents, and authorities there might be at a given moment. Viewing the trends of cities, of states, and of modern nations, and considering the nature and logic of management, we cannot escape the conclusion that the form of the near future will include the general type of organization suggested by the Committee.

Dean Landis regards this feature of the President's Committee's Report as especially ill-founded. He says:

"Only a year ago a distinguished group of scholars, reporting to the President of the United States

— in language hardly indicative of academic re-
straint — described the independent administrative
agencies of the federal government as constituting
'a headless "fourth branch" of the Government, a
haphazard deposit of irresponsible agencies and
uncoördinated powers,' whose institution did 'violence to the basic theory of the American Constitution that there should be three major branches of
the Government and only three.'

"Such apotheosizing obscures rather than clari-
fies thought. Despite this chorus of abuse and
tirade, the growth of the administrative process
shows little sign of being halted. Instead, it still
exhibits the vigor that attends lusty youth, and, if
we have defined our subject rightly, it is a youth
with which we are concerned. For here is an institution that has existed for less than a century
and which with a few exceptions has been of public
moment for only a little more than half that time.
Yet, its extraordinary growth in recent years, the
increasing frequency with which government has
come to resort to it, the extent to which it is cre-
ating new relationships between the individual, the
body economic, and the state, already have given
it great stature." [1]

Professor Corwin declares in his scholarly book:

"In other words, the world of administration is a
pluralistic rather than a *monistic* world, and reposes

[1] James M. Landis, *The Administrative Process* (1938), pp. 4-5.

on the loyalty and competence of individual bu-
reaucrats, qualities which thrive best in conditions
making for independence of judgment and pride in
a job well done. Certainly, to conceive of the
President as a potential 'boss of the works' save in
situations raising broad issues of policy would be
both absurd and calamitous; and for such issues the
legislative process is still available, a field in which
presidential leadership is today a more vital factor
than ever before. At the same time, however, it is
not even today the only factor; and the Committee's complaint that the commissions produce
'confusion' and 'conflict' 'in the execution of the
President's policies' is, consequently, only partly
valid. For the broader policies which these commissions were created to carry out are laid down in
the law itself, in the making of which Congress still
shares." [1]

Both of these worthy gentlemen seem to have
misunderstood the nature of administrative management in a going concern. This is often a lawyer's
view, without roots in the developing science or
art of administration. We went all through this
period of misunderstanding in regard to taxation,
more recently in regard to civil service, and now
are going through it in the area of administrative
management on a larger scale. The proper conception of the executive is precisely what Professor

[1] Corwin, *The President*, p. 359.

Corwin calls "absurd and calamitous" — namely, as the director of the works in the area of management. Otherwise we have a headless enterprise.

Of all the groups whose rethinking of the relation between the ends and the means of democracy is important, the legal profession is preëminent. Whether or not Dean Burgess' early characterization of the government of the United States as the "aristocracy of the robe" was or is accurate, it must be conceded that the bar is the most powerful single group dealing with the daily operation of the political association. Justice is in the lawyer's hands. The largest group of lawmakers is made up of the lawyers.

It is in the field of administration that the chief problem arises. The art and science of public administration or administrative management is the latecomer in the area of politics. Most lawyers are not trained in administration or even in administrative law, though this latter now becomes more general. The borderlines of legal justice and administrative management are to many lawyers, as well as to many laymen, a *terra incognita* — but not an unknown land into which they fear to rush.

But the application of the standard techniques of law to the emerging problems of administration is fraught with many difficulties, and the way is strewn with many disasters. The adjustment of a problem by two lawyers and a judge, if all are incompetent in administration, is the formula for misunderstanding and probably for mistake. In some areas this difficulty has been met and overcome. In the Civil Service, for example, we went through a sad period. Under the guidance of those whose training was not in administration but in private law, in many instances the removal of an incompetent civil servant was conducted as if it were a criminal proceeding. The maladjusted public servant was tried as if he were charged with a misdemeanor or a felony, with an attorney for the defense and a prosecutor conducting the hearing before a like-minded attorney. In the course of time these difficulties have been overcome, although by no means completely yet, and an administrative procedure is now generally recognized and accepted.[1]

But in many other areas the development of administrative discretion, along with the struggle for administrative competence, gave rise to many problems. The recent difficulties with the National Labor Relations Board illustrate some of the difficulties that arise when old-time legalism meets the new-time development of collective bargaining. At this very time sundry measures undertake to provide a type of judicial review, doubtless with the best of motives, which would cripple administra-

[1] *Report of Attorney General's Committee on Administrative Procedure*, 1941.

tive efficiency and would make impossible dynamic
government in a dynamic day. I do not question
the motives of the authors of such an undertaking,
but I cite their ill-timed efforts as an outstanding
illustration of the importance of thinking through
the essentials of action in the form of political association we call "democracy." Over-restriction
might properly be called the "kiss of death" to
modern types of technical competent administration. For no government without competent administration can survive.

Measures for undue restriction of administrative
authority would seriously cripple the development
of administrative authority under legislative direction by providing for judicial appeal in a wide range
of impossible cases. However well-intentioned
such restrictions, they would seriously hamper the
operations of government, and, one may safely
predict, would be modified either in practice or by
repeal or by wise judges on the bench. But in the
meantime the interests of the state would suffer,
as well as the interests of the whole community.

I cannot refrain from observing that some of
the driving force behind a few of these measures is
not the desire to attain an administrative or legal
objective, but to prevent effective governmental
regulation of various special interests — a part, in
short, of the struggle for general regulation of economic concentration. But if this is true, the menace

to democracy is even greater. The one might indicate a difference regarding details of management; but the other is a difference regarding the relation of the general good to private interests and private goods.

Future of Administrative Management

Public administration at this critical moment is of greater importance than ever before. With startling and incredible rapidity, volcanic changes have swept over the world, smashing at the ways of life and thrusting upon us urgent problems of the most fundamental type. Many of these problems depend for their solution upon skill in administrative management.

The democratic national state finds itself ringed around by hostile forces vowing the extermination of democracy and the reduction to practical slavery of its peoples, ruthlessly and pitilessly. This aggression contemplates the destruction of its rivals after a manner not merely military but political, not merely political but economic, not merely economic but cultural: a total demolition and destruction of all that stands in the way of a military imperialism which has equipped itself with weapons of modern technology, from chemical explosives to propaganda and mass psychology.

This challenge to America and to the democratic national states summons the use of every energy at our command, in the most effective manner possible. Both external affairs and internal relations will be subjected to the very severest strain, and will test to the limit our capacity for readjustment to the realities of the modern struggle for life. Among the ways and means of survival in this fateful hour administrative management will loom large — if not the largest single factor in the death grapple we now face. What we encounter is not just another "interesting problem" but a bloody clash with grim reality. What we are swiftly approaching — are now actually in — is a new era in national and world affairs. This is a revolutionary period — almost a preview of Armageddon.

By reason of the Axis blackout of free institutions, the planning of national defense is an urgent problem, opening out new and difficult situations of many kinds arising from new forms of "total war." Unless an early and decisive defeat is inflicted upon the Axis powers, we must contemplate far-flung warfare, declared or undeclared, military, economic, diplomatic, of a new and total type, hitherto unfamiliar to mankind. This contest will involve a sweeping reorientation and reorganization of administrative practice in many directions by keen and energetic minds, many of whom will be administrators. There will be drawn into consideration and use new forms of fiscal and economic administration capable of mobilizing our national resources and those of other free states to meet and overcome the tactics of such Schachts and others as may from time to time arise. In these titanic struggles, public administration will be of vital importance and will enter intimately into military-civilian problems, into over-all fiscal administrative problems of a new category, into realistic reorganization of our full national capacities, into devices enabling us to deal effectively with inter-American and indeed global relations among free states.

There are at least three important phases of this new development: (1) that of military mobilization for defense; (2) that of mobilization of all national resources (human and material) for national defense; (3) that of the post-emergency situation dealing with demobilization and restabilization of military, economic, and social activities. In each of these stages the type of administrative management affects vitally the ways of life. General policies, it is true, will come from the policy-makers, but much of the initiative for and correction of these policies will come from the practical experience of administrators. Further, the success of a policy once determined upon will depend in large measure on the skill and reliability of the administrators to whose care the application of the policy is entrusted. In dealing with social forces moving with incredible velocity, as at the present time, the judgment and capacity of the administrator on the job will inevitably be of very great moment.

A military emergency calls at once for administrative skills of the highest order, not merely in the narrower domain of military affairs as such, an enormous task in itself, but in the readjustment of many related matters of civil administration. For example, the dependents of soldiers immediately present a problem of the adjustment of the present civilian forms of social security to military provisions. The recruitment, reallocation, and training of industrial forces to meet the new demands for war materials bring problems, largely administrative, regarding the location of industries, housing, health, wages and hours. The experience of our last war showed the significance of administering wisely the necessary allocations and priorities of materials and men in the strenuous emergency effort to organize the national resources in the most effective manner. Almost every home, every farm, every industry, every school is affected directly by the mobilization for war or preparation in view of the threat of war. The government is expected to cushion the shocks of change upon the individual, upon the family, upon the school, the church, industry. Weaving together the extraordinary military efforts and the regular activities of society is itself a major problem in skillful administration.

But the kind of world struggle now breaking

upon us involves far more than the old-time mobilization of an army and its distant support with
men, munitions, and provisions. Modern war
places the civilian population in the front line of
defense. Civilian as well as military administration
is called upon for personnel, plans, management of
situations as in London and Berlin, which are not
described in the books. Invention and improvisa-
tion are imperative. There may be no time for
legislatures to convene or for courts to decide.
Competent and energetic administrative staff must
carry the load for the time.

But our modern contest is fought not merely with
military weapons of the old and new types, but
with economic explosives as well. Organizational
devices are now directed toward the mobilization
of the entire resources of the nation against forces
aiming to annihilate or subdue us. Export-import
control, systems of barter, blocked currencies,
manipulated exchanges and credit instruments are
types of the means in question; and these devices
in turn rest upon administrative management of men
and materials.

Total national forces assembled in massive fashion
and directed against individual nations are difficult
to withstand. We do not propose to adopt totalitarian principles or methods based upon them, but
in order to defend ourselves successfully we must
contrive our own policies of counterattack. Our

new democratic policies will call for administrative management of very high quality — superior personnel, superior fiscal management, superior planning, superior methods and practices — blending together the highest available skills of industrial management, military management, public administration; and summoning ability to meet emerging situations for many of which there will be found no precedents.

One instance like that of the disposition of the surplus commodities of the Americas illustrates clearly the vast importance of administration and the possibilities for muddling. Furthermore, a series of local adjustments must be made all along the line to these major external policies. All this becomes far more complicated and difficult with the intensity of the new international struggle which may precede actual war of the older type, and may long outlast it.

The third phase — namely, demobilization of emergency efforts and the return to stabilization again — is likewise a task of fundamental importance, a task to which we must look forward and for which we must plan before the new situation leaps out at us and demands a solution, *instanter*.[1] Our general staff must be prepared for all emergencies with alternative plans and courses of action ready for use. And certainly a return from the

[1] See Chapter V.

emergency must be anticipated —if not soon, then in the not too distant future. Returning soldiers, returning civilians must be aided back to stabilization. Returning capital, labor, and agriculture are problems of magnitude. Factories, farms, mines, stimulated to emergency production, must be re-adjusted to another scale or other uses found for them. Production and consumption must be balanced again. Part of this problem is, of course, a matter of national policy; but skillful planning administration will be necessary to deal with these policies, when men and machines come back to a base of life other than the struggle for bare national survival.

At such points, the interrelations of army administration, civil administration, and private administration are of the highest consequence to the welfare of our citizens. Without sound management, the structure of society will bog down, but skilled personnel and practices will aid immeasurably in reconstruction and readjustment. Otherwise peace may bring calamities as hard to bear as those of war or a war-tension period.

In all these emergencies, experience shows that the instant cry is for personnel, skilled personnel, and more personnel, and experience shows how high enterprises sag down and perhaps fall for lack of the necessary administrative capacity. It is in the light of such considerations as these that we view the question of the importance of public administration in our time.

I am saying nothing here about the burdens imposed upon us by the ordinary requirements of administrative management in dealing with the complicated problems involved in the adjustment of human needs to the amazing development of technological instrumentalities of countless types. The problems of administration are far from solved in these large areas of human behavior. Even without any emergency, public administration is of far-reaching importance as an instrument for the facilitation of social and political needs, but with the added burdens of an all-time emergency its meaning becomes far greater and yet more challenging.

These emergency aspects of modern administration, not to speak of wide-ranging internal problems of readjustment, indicate clearly the urgent necessity of a major concentration of interest upon the underlying problems of administrative management. There is no inherent conflict between high ideals of democracy and high administrative capacity. On the contrary, they are rooted in the same fertile soil of reason and faith in the future. But it is important to see to it that nothing stands in the way of their union.

This is no time for halfway or halfhearted thinking, or anaemic policies and programs of action. A restless world is on its way, not knowing whither.

WILLAMETTE COLLEGE LIBRARY

perhaps, but under the leadership of reckless gorilla types who have been cunning enough to seize upon some of the weapons made by reason to use for their own mad purposes. On our part, this is an occasion for tough-minded thinking and hardboiled action. Not all the ills under which mankind suffers can be cured by better administration, but relatively few of them can be remedied without sound and competent modes of management.

Finally, the goal of administrative management is not the worship of a god of management as such. The true end is facilitating human effort and achievement. Good management provides an easier way of doing what otherwise is more difficult or cannot be done at all. Much organization is ineffective, it is true, and is found to be unpleasant, painful, irksome, oppressive, or obstructive. This means that diligent search must be made for the diagnosis that will reveal the malfunctioning of management and lead to the invention of superior ways of achieving our ends. If any type of administration does not aid the personality and serve the group, it is a dead weight to be cast off.

The goal of human aspiration is liberty — self-expression — the unfolding of human personality in constantly richer and more diverse forms. Except as it contributes to this advance toward a higher liberty, all administrative management is as sounding brass and a tinkling cymbal. Our democracy is not menaced by sound administration, but aided by it. On the whole, the strategy of organization, if soundly conceived, will ultimately increase rather than diminish the realm of the personality. The area of personal decisions could and should expand in a new world of far more complex relationship yet with indefinitely broader horizons than those of our ancestors.

CHAPTER III

Democracy and World Order

THE future of democracy for some time to come depends upon its external policy, upon its ability to maintain itself in a world ringed around with force, upon its ability to organize a world from which violence is excluded as a normal means of settling difficulties between states. Whatever happens now, democracy is an ideal form of political association which will never die, but will rise from the ashes of demolished hopes and again make its way among men. Long periods of suffering and frustration would be saved, however, if the free states of the world could now drive forward with enough power to secure a free world of free states with free ideals.

This cannot be achieved without national unity and without international understandings, without a willingness to sacrifice the means to the end, the petty to the fundamental, the personal to the common good. Let us look at some of the considerations involved.

There are two great objectives of democracies in the field of world relationships:

I. The security of a jural order of the world in which decisions are made on the basis of justice rather than violence.

II. The fullest development of the national resources of all nations and the fullest participation of all peoples in the gains of civilization.

I

The ideal area of organization supposes a jural order of the world. Most of the classical theory upon this point is not valid now, if it ever was. There cannot be free states unless there is a free world. This does not necessarily involve a world-state, but it supposes an end of anarchy between states and the organization of a world-order. It presupposes a common understanding of "aggression" and a common method of enforcing the world's ideas of aggression, of basic order, and of basic justice — some form of collective security.

There may be sovereign states in the world-order, but they will not be states from whose decisions there is no appeal in the hierarchy of justice. There may be sovereigns; but they will not be absolute, unlimited, and unreasonable. There cannot be tiny and isolated states of 5,040 persons, as Plato declared, or 10,000, as Aristotle set up (isolated), except in a world-order. There may be and will be wide areas of autonomy, political and otherwise; but they will not be areas of absolute isolation. The modern drive for world-organization is no longer merely the product of ethical hopes alone, or of generalized humanitarianism, but is also the mechanical fiat of revolutionized transportation, intercommunication, and production which have reduced the size of the world to its present shrunken dimensions and necessitated the reorganization of a larger-scale economy. The urge comes not only from the burden of competitive armament, but from the practical realization of the unpleasant consequences of world-anarchy, in which any mad aggressor may disturb the peace of all the others in his world. It takes many to make peace, but one alone may make war; and he may be stopped only by counter-war or force in some equivalent form.

A glance at an interesting brochure, *This Shrinking World*, by Dr. Staley, shows the astounding change wrought in the modern world:

Eotechnics — 1830–40 shows the best regular speed at 10 miles an hour.

Paleotechnics — late 19th and early 20th centuries, at 65 miles an hour on land and 25 on sea.

Neotechnics — present era — shows best regular speed in the air at 200 miles an hour.

And the next technics will raise this figure to double 200 and more.

What effect has this on the boundary lines of

modern national states?   As mobility becomes greater, exclusiveness becomes greater, curiously enough — and yet understandably enough too. Men are not free to go, when they could go; exclusions and quotas bar the way. But these limitations mark a transition period which will pass away with the social and economic and political recognition of the nature of the new world.

What the form of a jural world order may come to be we do not know. Many volumes have been written upon this problem, and others are in the making. We do know, however, the line of direction that runs from violence to reasonable adjustment and balance. That the Roman Empire, or the Holy Roman Empire, or the Holy Alliance, or in our day the League of Nations, did not permanently solve the problem does not prove that the problem is insoluble; nor does it afford adequate cause for permanent discouragement and futilitarian passivity. To assert that the failure of the League of Nations was due to inherent difficulties is for Americans especially in the nature of a grim jest. This is a "lie that has become a legend" — since the United States won the war, demanded the League, and then walked out on the peace, leaving the world to find its way out of the muddle. Instead, we outlawed war — on paper.[1]

But there are many other forms of jural associa-

[1] See Merriam, *What Is Democracy?*, Lecture V.

tions, and there is every reason to expect that plans and practical experiments will be tried in the coming generation. It may be necessary to try many ways before we find one that will lead us where we want to go, as in the formation of our Union — to the jural order of the world, to the real outlawry of war, not merely on paper but in fact.

At the present moment we are confronted with the problem of Inter-American relations, with the global problem of the larger jural order of the world, and with the relations between free democratic states of the world. These questions we can and should face without fear and with full confidence, if we are willing to assume a dynamic role instead of passively accepting a role of inferiority.

The global objectives are to advance the well-being of the human beings who inhabit the earth by affording them full opportunity to realize their individual and social potentialities, to derive the maximum satisfaction from the exercise of their creative talents, and to fulfill their spiritual aspirations. In broad terms, those global objectives might involve general access to the natural riches of the earth, the most advantageous division of labor and productive processes in terms of natural resources, climate, aptitudes and skills, with wide distribution of products in a free enterprise economy, free movement from place to place, universal freedom of

thought and expression, and opportunity to partici-
pate on terms of equality in social decisions.

These global objectives, you may say, seem far
removed from the present world. But there is a
new world in the making which is only vaguely
perceived. Already scientific invention has tele-
scoped time and space. Radio voices circle the
globe. The motion picture whisks multitudes on
its magic carpet to wide adventures. History in the
making marches before countless eyes with quick-
ening tread. Mass production sends its stream swirl-
ing out into the remotest corners. But all this is
merely the beginning. The world is waiting to
yield up untold new riches at the touch of science
and technology. By overcoming the remnants of
savagery and by surmounting ineptness in social
organization, this new world is obtainable.

We may say, then, that a basic assumption of
international planning is the common concern of
the free peoples, — as individuals, to continue to
live as free men, and, at the same time, as nations,
to continue to exist as free nations. Planning, then,
proceeds from that assumption to discover in what
ways it may be possible for the various peoples, as
free men and as free nations, to organize their
political machinery so as to facilitate the achievement of their common objectives.

There is a world citizenship in fact, though not
in law. In a sense, the very existence of our com-

mon concern creates a common citizenry composed
of all free men. This citizenship is of a quality also
shared by all those who are devoted to the principle of democracy. Of course, this kind of citizenship has no political recognition or legal status,
and for that reason may escape the notice of the
jurists; but for all that, it has long been sensed by
the politically discerning, and now that the threat
to democracies everywhere is so great and so immediate the feeling of common citizenship is practically universal.

Of course, plans for military defense, for economic readjustment and prosperity, for cultural
advance and for spiritual realization must take into
account the political organizations through which
the administrative machinery for carrying out the
plans may be provided. In this phase of planning it
will be necessary to consider the existing political
organizations — how well they are adapted to the
purposes of the program, what changes may be required to make the realization of the program easier,
and what organizational obstacles must be removed.
All of this, of course, must be done without infring-
ing upon the essential role of the individual or of
any one of the nations.

Some form of what may be called the higher
federalism, predicated upon common concerns and
some type of common citizenship, lies ahead. Absolute insistence upon sovereign independence, in

accordance with traditional conceptions of nationalism, even when coupled with strict neutrality, has not enabled nations, small or large, to safeguard either their national integrity or the liberties of their peoples. The events of the last year have proved all too clearly that free nations, acting independently, or even acting together under formal alliances of the nineteenth-century type, are vulnerable to the attacks of the combined strength of the anti-democratic powers.

A prime difficulty in undertaking even a preliminary exploration of the possibilities of the higher federalism is that the vocabulary of politics, in its commonly accepted definitions, lags behind political events. Many still are frightened at what they term the "imperialism" of the British Empire, although that Empire was dissolved into the British Commonwealth of Nations by the Statute of Westminster. The symbol of the crown and a common citizenship unite, but do not compel, the peoples of a British federation of nations. There is no adequate terminology with which to label many of the new political phenomena springing up before our eyes. We see, for illustration, that England offered to France, on the eve of its tragic collapse, an absolute union, with common citizenship, common defense, and common currency. If that offer had been made a little sooner, or if the French people had known about it when it was made, or if there had been sufficient political planning to have foreseen such a union, basic liberties now lost in the vast prison camp of France might have been saved. But the concept was so novel and came so suddenly that it was too late.

Again, the United Kingdom and the Dominion of Canada, acting in concert with certain British colonial possessions, gave to the United States the use of two British naval and military bases, and, in exchange for fifty United States destroyers, bartered the use of six more. That was done with the all but universal approval of the peoples of all the nations concerned, but without the requirement of a treaty or other convention of the traditional sort.

Following this unprecedented action of a sovereign nation, giving to another nation the free use of its military outposts, the United States extended the use of all eight of these military bases freely to twenty other individual sovereign nations. There is no accepted set of political words with which to label neatly either those unprecedented actions or the train of circumstances which has resulted therefrom.

If Australia and New Zealand join with the United Kingdom in offering the use of the British naval base at Singapore to the United States, will the United States, if it accepts, feel equally free to invite Brazil and Argentina and all the others to use it? If it be desired to open Singapore to the

Dutch navy, defending the Dutch East Indies, will the invitation proceed from London, from Canberra, from Wellington, from Washington, or from all four?

It is true that not all of the old political practices are abandoned, by any means. Germany and Italy, the Axis powers, join with Japan in an offensive-defensive alliance, which at one and the same time excused communist Russia and was directed against the democratic nations. This was accomplished in a formal pact signed with great ceremony in Berlin. But at the same time there is reason to believe that the ceremony was prized more for its dramatic values than for any legal validity that it might lend to the arrangements. Why bother about formal treaties and public shows? Certainly neither Germany nor Japan has felt any compulsion to abide by traditional forms of international law, since they have found it possible to abrogate treaties without formal denunciations, to say nothing of armed invasions of other nations without the formality of a declaration of war. Certainly their confederation based on opposition to democracy has resulted in united action the effectiveness of which is not measured by any treaty, convention, or statute.

Plans for the higher federalism, through which the machinery for making good the common objectives of the American and other nations might be set up, might be made without formal written constitutional changes. Rather, these plans could be adjustable from time to time, and be sufficiently flexible to enable necessary readjustment to be made quickly in accordance with developing needs. Actually, it is this type of coöperation that already is developing in the common defense plans for the American republics growing out of the conferences of Panama and Havana and the conversations between the United States and Canada. It is this higher coöperation that was envisaged in the Act of Havana when it provided for the expansion of the activities of the Inter-American financial and economic advisory committee, and when it set up the scheme for the Inter-American commission for territorial administration to guard against the transfer of territory of non-American nations in the Western Hemisphere.

In addition to such functional organization for common action, however, democratic planning may also require the exploration of bolder devices for political solidification without the sacrifice of national entity. Among new types of possibilities to be freely examined are various forms of common citizenship. The extension of the scope of citizenship or some new and original form of common civic rights to coincide with the area of joint action would give political validity to military, economic, and cultural programs now being undertaken or yet to be begun. This citizenship need not infringe upon either the privileges or the limitations of national citizenship. It might indeed be very restricted in its scope, symbolic as much as substantial, yet important and useful. For instance, citizenship in the United States does not carry with it the right to vote, the suffrage being bestowed upon citizens of the United States (sometimes upon non-citizens) by the several states, which are restrained only by the negative mandate that they may not deny the right to vote because of certain reasons. Citizenship, from one point of view, is a bundle of rights, privileges, and duties. Some common citizenship, broadly defined, might also serve to remove certain disabilities of alienage without affecting essential national control of migration.

It might be possible to minimize the difficulties caused by the existence of many national currencies (to say nothing of the circulating media of the French, British, and Dutch colonies). The project for an Inter-American Bank provides, among other things, for the amelioration of the exchange situation, and various suggestions have been made with respect to the refunding of external debts of some American nations by conversion into obligations payable in domestic currency. Whether the creation of a common currency is possible depends, of course, upon many political as well as economic factors. If the management of such a currency is not beyond possibility, there can be no question of its desirable features. But currency itself is only a symbol for a complex of intricate economic processes ranging over a broad field of exchanges of products, credit, production, prices, cycles, resources, development.

II

The next objective on the democratic agenda, after security, order, justice, is as a stated purpose: (a) the fullest possible development of natural and human resources in every community of the world; and (b) the general participation of the mass of the community in these progressive gains. This means an end of exploitation of nations by nations, a world operating on a fraternal rather than a differential basis, and an end of the passive acceptance of the slave role of great sections of mankind.

Democracy may make the desert grow, but must see to it that the inhabitants of what was once the desert share in what is grown. The democratic political association must take care that the conditions under which democracy may freely operate are developed and preserved against special privilege of every sort. A free-trade world is not enough, for freedom cannot operate among those who are under duress, either among nations or within nations. There should not be nations to whom Anatole France's phrase would be applicable — enjoying "the majestic equality of the laws, which forbid rich and poor alike to sleep under the bridges, to beg in the streets, and to steal their bread."

If anyone says this cannot be done in a day, my answer is that we have more than a day to complete the task. But it will help to find the way if we have the will to find it and if the principle is declared and accepted. And until this way is found the democratic world program will remain imperfect and incomplete.

In an economy of scarcity, when there was not enough to go around, some were pushed out to starve or suffer. Whenever pestilence and famine came, there was no answer to the bitter cries of the weaker. But in our day there is no reason for inadequate food, shelter, clothing, cultural opportunity. No answer except the inadequate organization of mankind, no answer except inability to face what is new and utilize it for the common good. We know that poverty and war are not the curse of God but the curse of man himself, slow to associate effectively with his fellow men and prone to permit the crystallization of momentary efficiency into permanent privilege.

Machinery for systematically planning the development and utilization of national resources, both physical and human, could be created by individual and by joint political action. A number of American nations have planning agencies of various types, but all are concerned with basic questions of national planning, as is our National Resources Planning Board. The higher federalism could be useful to all of the peoples of all of the nations in their planning, and that without encountering the difficulties in joint administration of operating agencies. This is true because the planning function is not authoritative and coercive, but advisory and persuasive in nature. It is relatively easy to interchange ideas and experience about planning of national resources. The Havana Conference (1940) set up an Inter-American Conservation Commission, upon which like commissions of the several American states might be represented; in the United States the NRPB has been designated as the representative of the United States. Doubtless in the near future these commissions will be called together for the consideration of their common problems of national resources and their development.

In conclusion, difficult as may be the planning problems we encounter in any approach to the higher federalism, it must be remembered that a certain measure of political organization is necessary to carry into effect the plans for coöperation in the fields of defense, economics, and culture. But it must also be remembered that there may be no independence for a democracy today except as a participant in a larger common scheme. Today it is more difficult than it was even a year ago to look forward to a world organization based upon a dominant community of democratic societies, a community of justice rather than of violence, dedicated to a jural order for the solution of difficulties through peaceful adjustment. Nevertheless, the ultimate goal of democratic planning must continue to be such a world organization. The impossibility of a complete scheme in the near future should not deter us from the development of the broadest and most inclusive framework that circumstances will now permit.

It is not my purpose to attempt here anything but the broadest considerations regarding the emerging world order. But this is on the agenda of democracy. A jural order of the world might conceivably be set up by the combination of democratic and non-democratic states, assuming a willingness to coöperate within the framework of a society built upon reciprocal assurances and institutions, upon international law and institutions. But aggression is more likely to come from the non-democratic states than from the democratic communities, which have reason and justice as their ideal rather than violence and war. In the long run we look forward to a world of free states in which all of the associates are concerned with the ends and means of democracy.

Just as democracy was once held to be impossible except among a small number of people and in a very restricted area, so it is now maintained that jural order can be obtained and secured only by the control of absolutistic states, such as the Axis powers — either one alone or several in combination — some balance of power in which order might be preserved. But although democratic systems of government were originally based on the assumption of a small territory and a small people, such as Athens or a Swiss canton, and the larger areas and numbers were relegated to non-democratic states, in recent times all this has changed. The liberal-democratic movement laid the foundations of modern Germany and modern Italy against non-democratic opposition, although these nations subsequently became reactionary. The United States of America has presented the case of a far-ranging territory developed under democratic auspices, and the British Commonwealth of Nations has likewise shown how a far-flung area may be developed under democratic rule. The impulse to the formation of the League of Nations was obviously a democratic one.

There is nothing incompatible between large-scale units and the democratic form of political association. There is no reason to conclude that military empire is the best way in which to unify diverse elements in terms of modern communication and transportation. Military conquest is one way, to be sure, but the after effects of conquest and the slow readjustments that must be made exact a far higher price for necessary or desirable unification than is required. The areas of autonomy and self-determination which are desirable may more readily be achieved through the democratic methods of persuasion and coöperation with a minimum of violence — itself a low-level form of organization. Fraternalism is more flexible than force as a basis for association, and it further provides elements of tenacity and persistence of the first order.

Within the framework of a democratic society, in short, the new organization of world order may develop most readily and endure most persistently. The results attained by force of arms are spectacular and impressive beyond their true significance, for in our day management and association are achieved primarily by education, coöperation, persuasion, participation. The cannon was the *ultima ratio regum*, but not the *ultima ratio* of a developing civilization with quite different modes of organization available to it than those of personal physical destruction. The firing squad, the prison, the straitjacket are methods of obtaining compliance to be sure, but they are not the methods indicated by our age of science. They are the relics of the age of misunderstanding and ignorance of the fundamental forces underneath human behavior. Weapons are open to democracy as well as absolutism, and may be and have been employed from time to time in order to make possible the pursuit of happiness in the paths of peace. But in the coming world order, violence will be reduced to a minimum, while education, persuasion, coöperation will be exalted as the ways of organizing human association for the attainment of its highest ends.

PART II
RECASTING THE PROGRAM OF DEMOCRACY

CHAPTER IV

Democratic Planning of National Resources

THE inner meaning of the democratic association is of supreme significance. Is democracy only the defender of an old and outdated order, it is asked, a cloak for old-fashioned and unbending capitalism, for pluto-democracy, for imperialism, for old style nationalism and the national balance of powers? Is there only form or procedure in liberty, justice, equality — form with the life squeezed out? Or is there vitality and soul in them? Have they possibilities for the future, or are they only useful for the student of the dead past? Is the present struggle one for the elaboration and intensification of the *status quo*, or is it the dawn of a new era of social justice?

These are questions that millions are asking in one form or another. Are we struggling for the glory, fame, profit, position, and prestige of a few? Is it for this we are enduring hardness? Or are we parts of a great movement for the emancipation of mankind, for new life bursting through the old-time shells?

If democracy heralds a new order, what are its general directives in modern terms? Will capitalism bend, or must it break? Will nationalism bend, or must it crash? Will racketeering, political or otherwise, mend its shabby ways, or must it be broken on the wheel of force? Can selfish elements entrenched according to the rules of the game blend their interests with those of the greater good, or will they pull down the pillars of the structure? [1]

Can any program be evolved which will so far satisfy conflicting elements as to make possible a unity strong enough and persistent enough to build for the future? Such unity will require concessions from labor, concessions from the farmer, concessions from business, big and little, concessions from the middle class, concessions from sovereigns, great and small, of many types.

The general principle underlying such a program is simple, but the execution is not so simple.

On the agenda of democracy there is, first, the systematic validation of the basic assumptions of democracy, and particularly the validation of the assumption that the gains of civilization are mass gains and should be shared in accordance with the principles of social justice.

It cannot be too strongly stated that one of the primary methods of validating the assumption that the gains of civilization are essentially mass gains

[1] See Francis Williams, *War by Revolution* (1940).

and should be distributed throughout the community as rapidly as possible is the *deliberate, continuing, systematic analysis of civilization's gains in a commonwealth, the mode and range of their distribution, the continuing enlargement of national income, and the consequent adjustment of mass gains to total gains.* The underlying principle is more important than the particular mechanisms or methods adopted.

A wide range of differentials is not precluded by such a policy. But the relation of differentials in reward to differentials in capacity must be faced openly, and the necessary adjustments must be made from time to time. If the process is continuous, the necessary modifications may be made with a minimum loss of morale and efficiency. In such an adjustment violence, hypocrisy, chicanery are least useful, whereas collection and analysis of basic data, interpretation of them, and foresight in planning are of the highest value. And, I may add, decision and resolution in action.

This involves the organization and operation of techniques for the advisory formulation of plans and programs designed to promote the fullest equitable use of our national resources.

I propose now to deal:

    i. With the techniques of planning for democratic programs.

    ii. With some of the basic problems of planning.

I

What are our national resources, it may be asked? The national resources consist of a variety of elements:

1. Our land, water, minerals, energies, productive equipment in many forms, dwellings and other physical equipment.

2. Our population itself, with its differing skills and faculties.

3. Our vast array of organizations and associations for the conduct of affairs, governmental, industrial, agricultural, cultural, religious, educational, and the operational understandings in which they are set.

4. Our American ideals, objectives and general directives.[1]

The mere cataloguing of these resources indicates an unequaled wealth of present and potential capacities. Impressive as is the review of our material resources and massive as their totals are, they are not the greatest of our assets. The dynamic energy of our people, our ingenuity in invention, our facility in organization, our courage and resourcefulness — these are our greatest treasures. These are more significant than our broad fertile lands, our masses of gold, our vast reserves of minerals,

[1] Some of these have been very briefly described in *Our National Resources*, prepared by the NRPB (1940).

our great manufacturing and transportation systems. America has become a symbol not only of
wealth and power, but of human hope for a richer
and finer life, opening out to men who are willing
to work together in democratic association for the
common good.

What is Planning?

Planning is an organized effort to utilize social
intelligence in the determination of national policies.
Planning is based upon fundamental facts regarding
resources, carefully assembled and thoroughly analyzed; upon a look around at the various factors
which must be brought together in order to avoid
clashing of policies or lack of unity in general direction; upon a look forward as well as a look around
and a look backward. Considering our resources
and trends as carefully as possible, and considering
the emerging problems, planners look forward to
the determination of long-time policies.

Many of these plans will be imperfect. Some will
be mistaken. But taken in its entirety, all planning
effort amounts to an intelligent forecast of the
nation's future, as carefully prepared as is possible
from the technical side, and as prudently as possible
from the point of view of community determination of community policies, local, state, and national.

From the beginning of our national life various
forms of planning have been in evidence. The in-

dustrial situation confronting the founders of this republic was one of widespread distress, insecurity, and depression of the most anxious type. They deliberately planned a way out, when most men held that even government could not be planned. The Constitution itself was an economico-political plan on a grand scale, not only providing a democratic frame of government, but also setting up special plans for dealing with currency, tariffs, interstate commerce, and international relations. Justice was the first term in the preamble and liberty the last, but between them came the general welfare, common defense, and domestic tranquillity. The Constitutional Convention itself was a large-scale planning board.

Alexander Hamilton's well-known *Report on Manufactures* presented in 1791 was an impressive consideration of national policy in industry and related fields of American interest. In broad terms Hamilton set out the national problems of economics and government and suggested specific lines of policy to be followed. The report on internal improvements drawn up by President Jefferson's Secretary of the Treasury, Albert Gallatin, was almost equally notable. Henry Clay developed later (1820) the famous "American system," in which tariff and internal improvements occupied a conspicuous place. It is clear that the encouragement of manufactures by a policy of protection began as a systematic planning procedure, though later it degenerated at times into a free-for-all scramble for favors.

The land policy of the United States was planned with similar deliberation. It began with the abolition of the system of primogeniture and entail, the basis of the British system of political and economic power. The "grand plan" of John Quincy Adams for the management of the national domain was not followed; but the later development of the American homestead policy (1862) was designed to give a homestead at a nominal cost to practically all prospective settlers.

Our public educational policy rested in large part upon the broad grants of public lands given — two sections per township — for school purposes, with additional amounts for land-grant colleges. All this was notable national planning as of that day and age, democratic in purpose and method and highly successful in producing results. Those who prefer not to call this planning may, of course, apply some other term, but that will not change the spirit and temper of the work of the first great national planners who laid broad foundations for the republic of their dreams. Down to the Civil War, no country in the world had made bolder and more successful experiments in the field of government and economics alike than the United States.

Following that war, planning centered for several decades in large-scale private industries, such as had scarcely been known theretofore. Giant enterprises began to dominate whole areas of industry, and to operate them in increasingly unified and systematic fashion, although not always in the public interest. But national planning did not cease. It was resorted to whenever the public came to believe that unrestricted business enterprise failed at some point to promote the national welfare. Examples of government action designed to protect public interests are the establishment of the Interstate Commerce Commission in 1887, the passage of the Sherman Antitrust Act of 1890, the organization of the Federal Trade Commission, and a long series of national and state measures having the same general purpose.

Another step toward national planning was the development of the conservation program designed for the protection of natural resources, under the leadership of Theodore Roosevelt. This wide-ranging movement constituted a striking example of intelligent and forward-looking national policy, designed to protect and promote our common interests through various types of controls preventive of wasteful exploitation of our basic resources. In addition to the plans of the United States Government, similar systems and arrangements were set up by several of the states in various fields.

A more dramatic development of national planning was the "economic mobilization" developed during the World War through the War Industries Board, the War Trade Board, the Shipping Board, the War Labor Board, the Food Administration, the Fuel Administration, and the Railroad Administration, with their various subsidiaries. Under the stimulus of the war objective and national unity of purpose, far-reaching plans were made for the utilization of resources, for the ordering of industry, and for the focusing of the nation's strength in military and naval pressure. Nor did plans for economic mobilization end with the war. The National Defense Act of 1921 is a plan for a national war emergency — a plan which covers the wide ranges of industrial life necessarily reorganized for war purposes.

Though the war-time controls were released promptly after the armistice, the speculative boom of 1919–20 and the severe though brief depression of 1920–21 brought home to everyone the fact that peace has her defeats no less than war. The elaborate report on *Waste in Industry*, sponsored by the American Engineering Council in 1921, was a landmark in a movement toward better economic management, and this line was followed by important developments of planning in the Department of Commerce. Trade associations began their rapid growth under the benevolent auspices of the United States Government. Attacks upon waste, demands for standardization, simplification, research in production efficiency, long-time plans for stabilization and equilibrium in industry, were pressed forward.

Another notable development was the reorganization of the budgetary procedure of the United States Government through the Budget Bureau and the Director of the Budget — a reform long advocated and finally accomplished — under President Harding. While many of these powers were already in the hands of the President, the deliberate planning of ways and means for the exercise of his authority unquestionably had an important influence in the direction of systematic scrutiny and control over public expenditures. The Federal Reserve Bank was set up to be an important agency for equilibrium in the field of banking and credit. The organization of the Federal Employment Stabilization Board through the efforts of Senator Wagner and President Hoover was an attempt to plan expenditures for public works over a period of years in relation to business cycles.

Meanwhile many forms of planning appeared. City planning agencies sprang up, reaching now the number of some one thousand. County planning boards have been established covering a quarter of our three thousand counties. Some forty-five state planning agencies have been established.[1] Regional

[1] For history of state planning, see Clifford J. Hynning, *State Conservation of Resources* (1939); R. A. Walker, *The Planning Function in Urban Government* (1941).

planning committees have been set up and commissions on interstate coöperation have been organized by most of the states. Many large-scale efforts in the field of planning have been developed by the United States Government in the last ten years, beginning with the Reconstruction Finance Corporation, the Home Owners' Loan Corporation, and the Federal Employment Stabilization Office under President Hoover. President Roosevelt initiated a broad sweep of policies in the field of social legislation. No effort is made here to sum up all of the attempts made in this direction.

Wide ranges of social legislation have been directed at regulation of industrial maladjustments. Sometimes these efforts took the form of labor legislation and sometimes they were aimed at the correction of corporate and other industrial abuses.

Notwithstanding differences of judgment regarding either the policy or the administration of these undertakings, there is general agreement that many of them have been highly successful. Taken together they illustrate the importance of planning our fundamental national policy in the emergency period upon which we are now entering. Doubtless many other evidences of national planning of resources both natural and human will be seen. It becomes more and more evident that the fullest use of American national resources cannot be obtained without careful and intelligent planning — national, state, and local.

The National Resources Planning Board, created by President Roosevelt in 1933, was substantially the projection of the Advisory Council recommended by President Hoover's Committee on Recent Social Trends, 1933. This body has made many studies of our physical and our human resources. The basic data regarding land use, water use, energy resources, long-time planning of public works, have been assembled by technicians and carefully analyzed, and various indicated policies have been suggested. In each of these areas broad programs have been outlined. Elaborate analyses have been made of the structure of our national economy, of consumer expenditure, and of consumer income. Reviews of industrial trends and their relation to employment stabilization, analyses of industrial-plant location, thoroughgoing scrutiny of our relief policy, and indications of a long-time method of procedure have been prepared and presented to responsible officials. More recently the Board has undertaken the preparation of plans for the post-emergency period on a considerable scale.

Fundamental inquiries have been made into basic factors in the national economy: scientific studies of population trends, of inventions and their social implications, of research as a national resource — research in government, in industry, in university centers. In addition to printed reports, many of the results are in the form of interoffice memoranda, and in the shape of private reports and memos submitted to the Executive. These taken together constitute an important section of the work of the planning agency on whatever level of government it may be found. An advisory agency will find that much of its advice is rejected in whole or in part, but this is one of the ways in which advisors are distinguished from the responsible policy-determiners or administrators dealing with operative activities. Advice often advances through roundabout and even underground channels. There may come a moment when the advice long since given comes back with a request for a review by the one who gave it.

One of the functions of the NRPB has been to serve as a clearinghouse for the several planning agencies of the country, local (urban-county), state, regional, interstate, and also private or quasi-private planning agencies in industry or elsewhere. Pioneer studies have been made in urbanism and in regionalism.[1] Help has been given by the encouragement of state planning boards of which there are now forty-odd, of county planning agencies, of interstate commissions on coöperation, fostered by the Council of State Governments. Finally the NRPB has aided in the establishment of nine re-

[1] *Our Cities* (1937); *Regional Factors in National Planning and Development* (1935).

gional agencies dealing with the planning problems of the larger regions of the United States.[1]

From the organizational point of view the NRPB is part of the Executive Office of the President.[2] This includes the White House Office, the Bureau of the Budget, the National Resources Planning Board, the Office of Government Reports, the Liaison Office for Personnel Management, and the Office for Emergency Management. With reference to other federal agencies outside of overhead management, the Board has endeavored to encourage planning activities in the various departments of the government. There is now a planning division, specifically so called, in the Department of Agriculture. There is one in the making (provided Congress gives an appropriation) in the Federal Works Agency; there is a general committee in the Department of the Interior which is not called a planning committee but which may serve the same purpose; and there are planning divisions in the War Department and in the Navy Department. There are similar enterprises not labeled "planning" but doing much the same work in a variety of other agencies, as, for example, in the Treasury, in Commerce, in the Federal Reserve Board, and in other independent agencies. The

[1] See report of 1941 containing the programs of these regions in the first stage of their development.

[2] See "The Executive Office of the President" in *Public Administration Review*, vol. I, no. 2, 1941.

Board has endeavored to make a special connection with federal agencies through its various technical committees, dealing with particular topics assigned by the President. These committees usually have representatives of several federal agencies, as, for example, the Committee on Long-Range Work and Relief Policies.

The National Resources Planning Board has undertaken to bring together partial plans made elsewhere and to join together agencies for central planning under circumstances where otherwise it would be very difficult or almost impossible. Each agency naturally plans and should plan for activities within its own jurisdiction. It is the function of the Resources Board to clear these plans or programs so that they do not run afoul of each other, to piece together plans that otherwise might not fit together, and to take an over-all view different from that of the special operating agencies charged with particular and specific responsibilities. Examples of such coördination of plans are the development of the multiple use of water instead of the single uses planned through a series of scattered agencies dealing with water; the land retirement and reclamation policy, which obviously interests two of the departments and many other agencies; a long-time program for public works, which spreads over and involves the coöperation of practically all of the agencies of the government; the long-term relief policy; and the development of population studies.

The National Resources Planning Board also deals with local agencies and particularly with the state planning boards. There are now about forty of these planning boards, some of them operating more vigorously and some of them less vigorously. They have survived the storm of political mutations and hardly anyone now raises the question in most cases whether the state planning board is a Republican or a Democratic institution. There are about as many of one type as of the other.

The NRPB has also endeavored to deal with regional planning groups. It has aided in setting up nine regions for planning. The Pacific Northwest Regional Planning Commission is perhaps the best-known group of this type, although the Tennessee Valley Authority is a grand example of a different form of regional planning in another style of operation. The Board has also established important relationships with the Council of State Governments and with the various commissions on interstate coöperation.

The Board has also dealt with private agencies interested in planning. The most notable example is its Science Committee. Here groups were brought together that never came together before, namely, the National Academy of Sciences, the Social Science Research Council, the American Council of Learned Societies, and the American

Council on Education with its twenty-seven con-
stituent organizations. The members of the Science
Committee are designated by these four groups.
These scientists have undertaken with the United
States Government some very important studies,
notably the study of population, the study of the
social implications of technology, and the study of
research as a national asset — research in the national
government, in private industry, and ultimately in
the various local governments.

The planning function is, of course, advisory in
its nature, with no power to command or to give
orders. In the report of the Committee on Administrative Management it was suggested that there
be three joint congressional committees correspond-
ing to the three agencies of over-all administrative
management: budget, personnel, and planning. It
was suggested that through these agencies Congress
might get a very clear and a very quick view of
what was happening in the field of overhead administrative management. This suggestion has not
yet been carried out.

II

Of all these basic types of national planning it
may be asked which loom the largest at the present
time?

First in order is the ending of world anarchy and
the establishment of a jural order within the frame-

work of which human relations may be conducted with a minimum of aggression and violence.

The twin problems next in rank are the increase in national production-expansion of the national income and the guaranty that these gains shall be fairly diffused throughout the community, promptly and in accord with recognized categories of social justice, in a fraternal rather than a proprietary spirit.

The problem of the most effective form of land use is fundamental in national policy and is yet far from settlement on a just and permanent basis.

The joint problem of industrial-labor organization, management, and regulation is a standing challenge to intelligent planning, but thus far contains a wide variety of factors upon which data and decisions must yet be found: the best size of the industrial unit, the establishment of security and justice for the worker, the respective roles of government, proprietorship, management, and workers — these are problems upon which the future of productivity and of justice alike depend.

A youth policy is close upon us and important decisions must soon be made involving army, industry, labor, and school points of view.

All of our national policies and plans will come to naught unless we are able to develop practical programs regarding such neglected elements of our national strength as population resources and research resources — elements which it is no longer possible to take for granted.

Our population will shortly come to a standstill unless new factors come in, and its distribution will be far different from that of the present day. There will be a vastly increased population in the older groups and a correspondingly smaller population in the younger age groupings. These simple facts alone involve far-reaching changes in the structure and functions of the American economy. How large a population do we want? what distribution of population shall we encourage? what care shall we take to ensure the soundest health and vigor of our population as we go along?

Research is one of the nation's greatest resources — an activity vital to national growth and development. Over $400,000,000 a year is spent on research work. The number of patents is running now about 50,000 a year. What are the social effects of these new discoveries in research and new inventions applying scientific results to everyday life? Here we come upon a vast problem of absolutely fundamental importance in the life of the state; for if invention stops, the growth of the nation slows down. To some it may seem absurd that a nation should plan a research policy, remote from everyday practical affairs. Yet this is absolutely vital to the development of a civilization or of a political society, whether in peace or in war. Social discovery and invention are as important — at this time more important — than discoveries in the field of natural science. Education, medicine, engineering are full of meaning for any people, and discoveries of new methods of management and association are equally significant. In view of the fabulous discoveries in science which lie ahead of us, it is all the more important that we be prepared to utilize these inventions as promptly as possible and make them effective in the daily life of our citizens. But we cannot utilize these magical discoveries unless we are prepared to adapt them to our ways of life freely and without sabotage of science.

But is not all this equivalent to "economic planning"? No, the term is too broad at one point, and too narrow at another. A planned technology or a planned education is more important than a planned "economy." The "economic" has been much over-emphasized in the discussions of human association, and we shall find it necessary to do our planning in different terms from the transactions of the market place, important as these are. Planning involves ranges and levels of values that are not within the purview of what is ordinarily regarded as "economic." The modern problem is a social problem rather than an economic one — national in the broadest sense of the term rather than industrial in the narrower. The fluid nature of money as a claim for services, commodities, and recognition often obscures the immense mass of values that lies outside the pecuniary circle and overlooks even the uncertainty of "money" itself. Money is not the source of science, invention, technology, management, labor; its values depend on them in the modern order of things. Modern wealth and property are the creation of the technology of a machine age, which made and could unmake our civilization.

Our planning may well begin with the sources of our present power rather than the accidents of its application — with an analysis of the creative forces of modern civilization. National "production" is not merely, as many seem to suppose, the building of factories in which goods are made, but the production of a civilization out of which comes the skill to invent the machinery of the factory, and the skills to operate it after it is set up. In the largest sense of the term, planners must consider all the resources of the nation, and strive for the highest and best use by the community. All details are subordinate to this major directive. The assumptions of democracy as the framework of association and of science as the genius of production are the guide to planning.

At this point, however, we meet the assertion that "planning" is *per se* impossible. Occasionally, all "planning" is lumped together as "collectivism," or "creeping collectivism." Of course, if all kinds of "planning" as such are inherently impossible

under the operation of natural laws, then no form
of association can enter this forbidden field. All
efforts would prove futilitarian in the end. But
usually this position is abandoned, in view of the
vast amount of modern plan making in cities, counties, industries. Curiously enough, agricultural
planning is not usually reckoned as "economic"
even by planning critics — or public works, or
highways, or perhaps even railways and airways.
Retreat is made to a special definition of "planning" as "economic planning" or "totalitarian planning."

Democratic Planning

Much of the criticism of democratic planning is
made by those who have not clearly understood
either "democracy" or "planning." Of course, if
we assume that the community does not know and
cannot know what it wants, and if we assume that
drifting is better than planning, we will not want
either democracy or planning, much less the two
in combination.

We can plan for war and also for peace. We can
solve the basic problem of national production, the
problem of unemployment, the problems of social
security, if we have the will and vision to make a
common effort worthy of the emergency in which
we find ourselves. Our economy is not a closed
one. We can make our 80 billion income 100 bil-

lions and from that go on to whatever the optimum figure may be. And within the framework of free industry and free government we can make sure that our national gains are democratically applied.

This will involve planning, as will our whole world situation, but planning within the boundaries of free society, industrial and political. The unplanned society in our day will not survive the competition of our time. Some seem to forget that we can plan to be free as well as plan to be unfree. Planning nothing is the direct road to planning everything.

The common good does not call for complete uniformity in conduct but requires variation in things that are not common. Effectiveness is determined not merely by the complete concentration of the power to decide, but also by that general good will and coöperativeness without which wise decisions cannot be made, or, if made, cannot be carried out. It is true that in a moment of great crisis — as in pestilence, war, famine, flood, fire — unity is important. To some this unity may seem important not only for a crisis but as a continuous practice. In reality, however, concentration in an emergency rests upon the assumption of long-time coöperation. The old-time dictators "cashed in," so to speak, on habits of coöperation in the state.

Despotisms old and new, in many periods of the world's history, have built great monuments flat-

tering to their pride — great pyramids, great boule-
vards, great empires — and some of these monuments, built as they were upon cruelty, blood, hate,
and scorn of the humble man, stood for centuries,
and still stand like the pyramids. These despotisms
were not, however, concerned with the elevation
of all men, with the fair distribution of the gains of
the community, with raising the standards of human
living — material, intellectual and spiritual — with
the emancipation of the slave or the serf, or with the
unfolding of the possibilities hidden in the human
personality.

Our democratic planning is aimed at the highest
possible standards of national production constantly
expanded through the years, and at the translation
of national production into the lives of the mass of
our citizens. We plan, not for the glory of the
conquerors or the gratification of national hatred
or national pride, but for ennobling and enriching
the existence of our citizens and of mankind.

Instead of concluding that a democracy cannot
manage or plan, we know that the contrary is true:
namely, that the nature of the democratic association is best adapted to management and planning.
Coöperation is the key to efficiency in planning and
management, and coöperation is most richly obtained when those concerned with the common
welfare are consulted about the common good.
Coöperation, in the long run, will produce more

units of material and spiritual good than clubbing. According to the old phrase, "The strongest are never so strong but that they try to turn their might into right and obedience into duty." In democracy duty springs spontaneously from consultation and consent freely arrived at and freely given.

In government, as in industry, the strategy of the new scientific and technological world calls for less of violence, less of brutality, less of authoritarianism, and for more of coöperation and more of consent; less charity and more fraternity; less shooting and more persuasion; less drifting and more consideration and planning of objectives; and finally, more sound administrative management under immediate executive direction and under final legislative supervision and control.

CHAPTER V

Democracy's New Guaranties of the Pursuit of Happiness

THE machinery of democracy may so operate that the gains of civilization are widely and fairly distributed, including here the material goods and the non-material values as well. The details of effecting this result are subordinate to the ends in view. The basic understanding and determination is the seed, the root, the life from which the means spring and upon which they must depend. It is the special task of democracy to watch the gains of civilization and their diffusion, and to set up the ways of translating these gains into terms of democratic human living.

Beyond the mechanisms for consent and for the basic freedoms, and beyond the requirements of a program of national security, there are certain fundamentals which underlie a democratic program guaranteeing social justice. These are the charges on the national income. They are the basic investments of a nation. They are an underwriting of fair participation in the gains of civilization. What are these more specifically?

For everyone equal access to minimum security as well as to the adventures of civilization.

For everyone food, shelter, clothing, on an American minimum standard.

For everyone a job at a fair wage — if he is in the labor market — and a guaranty against joblessness.

For everyone a guaranty of protection against accident and disease.

For everyone a guaranteed education, adapted to his personality and the world in which he lives.

For everyone a guaranty of protection against old age.

For everyone an opportunity for recreation and the cultural activities appropriate to his time.

It is one of the basic assumptions of democracy that through the democratic process of self-government, of discussion and deliberation, decisions may be reached leading to the very highest welfare of the community, on a higher level and more enduring than through any competing process of aristocracy or autocracy. Practical experience indicates that these results may be obtained.

The first phase of the democratic effort is ordinarily that of overthrowing vested interests of one type or another — land, heredity, arms, wealth — and establishing a sound democratic regime. The second stage is more difficult, for it involves the continuance of the democratic attitude and process under new conditions. The problem becomes not merely the preservation of the *status quo* against counter-revolution, but the further development of the general welfare of the community.

In a rapidly changing period such as ours, with its incredible advances in technology, the task is far greater than in static periods. The gains of civilization accumulate from day to day in rapid sequence, and even with the best of intentions it is not easy to keep pace with the growth of modern techniques and to apply them promptly to the community welfare. If, as is inevitable, the intentions of all are not good, but favorable to the retention of special privileges, the difficulties are even more formidable.

The root problem of democracy in our day is to see that the gains of our civilization are fairly distributed and translated into terms of the common good without undue delay. These gains are not material alone; they consist of goods, but also of services and opportunities for the development of the human personality in many ways, some calculable and others imponderable. In a democracy they are set in the framework of the dignity of man and the consent of the governed as essential to the protection and development of the general welfare.

Democracy assumes the responsibility for applying social intelligence to the solution of this problem of ensuring the fullest possible application of human gains to the service of the common good;

for democracy is not primarily based upon economic forces or cultural forces, important as all these are, but is a form of association through which all of these factors may focus on the development and happiness of the personality and on the promotion of the general welfare, in whatever terms the community thinks of welfare. Democracy is not merely a mechanism through which personal development might possibly be achieved, but also one for facilitating the fullest development of personalities within the purview of the common good.

Democracy cannot stand still unless civilization stands still, and never was there more rapid change than now. In a quiet, rural community, whose folk were gathered on the Swiss hillsides in democratic assembly, the tempo was very slow and the number of readjustments relatively small. But in Switzerland and elsewhere the influx of new forces now necessitates many changes in many directions.

It is, however, one of the great advantages of democracy that changes may most readily be made on the principle of fraternal association. Authority does not depend on status in a democratic society. Status itself is subordinated to the general welfare. Improvements in the arts and sciences need not be opposed, delayed, or obstructed, since the gains made are the gains of the community itself. In aristocracies or autocracies a shift in the productive power of the community or in other essential features of the given time may prove disastrous to those in authority. But in a democracy the community is the beneficiary, no matter what advance may be made, or whose personal status may be altered. A free and democratic society is therefore the most readily adaptable and adjustable of all forms of political association.

Refusal to accept continuation of previous status as a basis for power or position is a feature of the democratic system which enables it to face change and adjustment without fear of consequences to a principle of authority or to a person or group in temporary authority. In this regard, democracy has the fearlessness and unconventionality of science, which refuses to accept traditions that new truth rejects. Systems depending on the past alone fear the light, for time may show that their values are outgrown and bring about their rejection. But the bulk of the community in a democratic system cannot be upset by any social gain, for it is their own gain, if properly shared by the society.

It cannot be too strongly stated that it is a primary part of the democratic program to examine the gains of civilization as they emerge and to make sure that the community is the beneficiary of these gains. This involves more than the recognition of a minimum standard of living. It involves the optimum standard of living under the given conditions. A higher reward may be given for differential abilities, provided the rewards do not imperil the others, as in the case of concentration of economic or other power to a point where it threatens the democratic political framework on which the association depends.

Analysis of our national income in the NRPB study of 300,000 family budgets reveals wide discrepancies, wider than are comfortable in a democracy and wider than is desirable when we consider the consumption of goods as well as their distribution. With a national income of 59 billion dollars, 13 million units in 1935–36 had incomes not exceeding $780, 13 million families had incomes from $780 to $1450, and 13 million families had the remaining part of the national income.

If now we break down the family budgets of these groups, more light is thrown on the differentials. Thus, for food, the lower one-third spent $300; the middle one-third spent $500; the upper one-third spent $800. As to savings, however, the analysis shows that the lower two-thirds saved nothing, while the upper one-third saved 7 billions.

Material betterments of this situation, far greater than in any other period, have been made in recent years through a variety of measures such as minimum wage laws, social security acts, health, housing, stimulation of the business cycle, elimination of maladjustments in agriculture, labor, business. But there still remains much to be done in bringing about a fairer diffusion of the gains of our time. In systems that rest avowedly upon the principle of inequality, such differentials may pass without notice, but in democracy regard for the dignity of mankind, for social justice, for a fraternal community, cannot allow these wide differences to stand as our idea of equity. Our unremitting effort must be directed toward constant elimination of these unjust conditions.

Through a combination of factors, by no means simple in their operation and in their interrelations, it comes about that we are not able to consume what we produce in the fullest measure desirable and possible. It has been estimated that the full use of our national resources would have produced 80 billions — on the old base of 59 billions. The figure is now set at 80–85 billion with 100–125 billion in the offing, and the technocrats will give you a far ampler figure, limited only by their own sense of moderation.

Here we enter, I must warn you, into a wilderness of opposing views, not to say shouts, of competing economists. Competition still remains among economic theorists at least. Whatever happens in industrial practice, there is no monopoly of economic theory — fortunately for the theorists, although sometimes baffling for the rest of us. One of the reasons why their logic and their statistics do not always meet is that the problem is not one of economics but of politics plus economics plus other social factors which insist upon being brought into the count. Perhaps the number 1 item on the democratic agenda should be a true Political Economy, without too wide an estrangement between Politics and Economics.

It is possible to make an analysis of the productive capacity of a nation and of the modes of further expanding the volume of production of commodities and services. Such a survey would present the volume of productivity as it is, and a picture of production as it might be with its possibilities more fully utilized. This development is not so simple as it might seem, since it involves the calculation of various factors of production in relation to each other. Nor are all of the satisfactions that enter into a social equilibrium susceptible of analysis by the statistician. These factors must be determined in another way.

Over against the survey of production there may be set a survey of the patterns of consumption — revealed by inspection of representative budgets or other modes of determining consumption, and their advance with advancing income. When this work is completed at any given time, it would show, some experts declare, (a) the actual production pattern over against the actual consumption pattern, and (b) the idealized production pattern over against the idealized consumption pattern. In the light of these estimates it might be possible to indicate new patterns and mark out new standards of living, within the new range of national production. This is important in a national policy directed toward expanding the national income and ensuring that the possibilities of life within the given economy are realized in practice.

If experts declare and we agree upon the essentials of living, and if production figures indicate that these standards are obtainable, then the next step is to make these possibilities effective in the lives of men by such measures as may seem feasible. What this task eventually involves is a scrutiny of the national income with a view to observing its distribution, the priorities in its allocation, and its possibilities of expansion. This would reveal what it is, if anything, that takes precedence over the fair essentials of human living; what it is that is more important than food, shelter, clothing, care, hygiene, security, education. Such a program rests, of course, on the assumption that the gains of a nation are essentially mass gains and should be diffused throughout the community, and that the community itself should be the final judge of the equity of the distribution of values in the nation.

In the United States, for example, this program might involve the development of American standards of living, guaranteed by America as to certain fundamentals. It goes without saying that such standards would be subject to review and revision from time to time, as significant changes occurred in the productive mechanism of the nation and raised or lowered the productive capacity of the community. Above this standard would be, of course, a broad variety of differentials over and above the basic minima. The standard itself would rise constantly in a developing technical civilization and important surpluses would be absorbed in this rising standard of life. I do not say that all this can be accomplished in a day, but this is a picture of the future. This is the goal, and it is not too far away.

Who will pay the bills? you may ask. Who pays them now? Many pay, but especially those who do not consume what they could consume within the limits of our free national economy. Higher American standards of living and free industry are not foes but friends. The expansion of national income will encourage enterprise, expand trade, and result in the development of the whole economy, still very far from realizing its rich possibilities. Nursing the consumers is not waste, within reasonable limits.[1]

Likewise the American standard of living and national defense are not inconsistent but complementary. Our resources properly organized are

[1] "There is that scattereth and yet increaseth; and there is that withholdeth more than is meet, but it tendeth to poverty. . . .
"The liberal soul shall be made fat; and he that watereth shall be watered also himself." Proverbs 11, 24.

such as to enable us to carry any ordinary defense burden and at the same time provide for the amenities of life. We can have guns and butter too with our resources and organization.

If the gains of civilization go downward in exceptional emergency times, and from whatever cause, the group goes down. But one of the bitterest causes of complaint heretofore has been that both in depression and in war the lower two-thirds of the population has borne the heaviest burdens, out of proportion to their fair contribution, and at the same time without prospect of relative gains when the upturn comes. It is on the agenda of democracy to end this violation of the basic assumption on which democracy rests — "Bear ye one another's burdens."

What is it on the national budget that takes precedence over standards of living, aside from national emergency calling for general and equal sacrifice? And how shall we explain this to those who feel that they have not a fair share in the gains of the world they help to operate? And why should we? Is it food that we lack in America? Well, no, we must reply. Is it materials for clothing and shelter that we lack in America? No; there is abundance of these commodities. Is it hands to work? No; there have been many idle, until the present emergency. Is it money to work? There is idle capital, bursting the bankers' coffers.

If America were a poor nation, without adequate resources in men and materials and skills, then we might say, "We are sorry — some more convenient day we shall look after all these things. In the meantime, patience — endure the fate imposed upon you by God and nature." But in the United States the fault is not in natural or human resources. The demand is for brains, for will, for courage, for inventiveness in social, economic, and political arrangements equal to the adjustments that could be made and some day will be made, and for general coöperation by persons and by groups. I may further say that not only might these arrangements conceivably be made but assert that without such arrangements our democracy is very seriously weakened and its life threatened. In this titanic world struggle, political forms alone cannot survive unless they are filled with a substantial content of life. The surviving systems of the world will be those that provide the highest standards of living, material as well as idealistic.

The key to this strength is not to be found in economics alone, or in science alone, or in force alone, or in politics alone; but in some new synthesis of idealisms and realisms. *Laissez-faire* and free trade are not strong enough to organize the oncoming generations of mankind, nor are the dogmatic totalitarianisms of our time any sounder in limb.

In the United States fortunately the nation is strong enough in resources and in traditions and ideals to work out a modern program, satisfying the difficult equation presented by the modern quantities of technology, economics, and politics — and in so doing, to set a world standard to which other states may rally. We readily recognize the importance of mobilization of our nation's resources in times of war or emergency. The question is, are we equally ready to recognize our possibilities in times of peace in the struggle against low living standards?

And do you speak as an economist, Mr. Merriam? someone may say. Or as politicist — or even as a political economist?

I speak as a democrat and a patriot, as one interested in planning. As a democrat, I see the value of democratic morale based upon genuine validation of democratic assumptions. As a patriot, I observe that our national security rests upon the high morale of a contented people; arms and the man alike depend upon a realization of social justice, upon a sense of participation in the gains of civilization, upon freedom and security spelled out in terms of the daily lives of men and women.

As a student of planning, I see the possibility of adapting our national resources to our national needs in peace as well as in war, in the development of national productivity and higher standards of living as a part of the same program. This is the bill of rights in modern terms. This is life, liberty, and the pursuit of happiness in the twentieth-century economy of abundance.

Even while our emergency production is just reaching its full volume, it is important to look forward to the period following our emergency activities and to plan for the necessary readjustments that must be made. At the end of the World War crisis there was a sudden abandonment of war activities and a quick return to civil life on a pre-war basis. This was termed "the return to normalcy." But it was too sudden and violent for the national health. There was a temporary exhilaration, but not for long. The consequences were first felt in the agricultural areas, where widespread deflation and collapse fell upon thousands of victims. The industrial world swept forward into an era of frenzied speculation which came to a sad climax in the debacle of 1929 and the years following. The national income dropped from 80 billions to 40 billions, and in a few years 200 billions, or roughly one half of the national wealth, was wiped out. With this deflation came the untold misery of millions of our people in every way of life. Important devices such as the Reconstruction Finance Corporation and the Home Owners' Loan Bank were advanced, but they were too late; and they were not strongly and boldly enough supported to stem the tide. Far more energetic and effective action began in 1933, but already terrible punishment had been inflicted upon the body politic and economic.

We do not know at what time the end of our present emergency measures may come, or under what circumstances our readjustment must then be undertaken. But this makes it only the more important that we look forward as far as possible and prepare plans for dealing with the emergency whatever it may be. As a good general staff is ready in advance with alternative plans for the army adapted to a variety of alternative situations which may arise, so sound national policy requires preconsideration and preplanning designed to break the shock of readjustment and prevent the evils of another depression.[1]

Serious problems will be presented on many fronts when the emergency is over. Army personnel will be demobilized, and thousands will be returning to seek employment. Civilian personnel occupied in defense and collateral industries will be obliged to seek other occupations in a great readjustment movement. Agricultural personnel will be involved in readjustment of several types. Industrial expansion, dislocating the normal process

---

[1] The President asked the NRPB to prepare the agenda for such a plan or plans, December, 1940. See *After Defense — What?* by NRPB (August, 1941).

of production, will require important reorganization of plants and capital concerned. Other uses must be found for both properties and men, and in this process many communities will be seriously upset unless careful precautions are taken to guard against unorganized reëstablishments.

Even if we knew just when the emergency would end and under what world conditions, it would be a very formidable problem to foresee and prepare for the transition. The complexity of the approaching situation makes it all the more important that as much planning as possible be pressed forward now.

Yet even the knowledge that the problem is not being neglected and that serious efforts are being made to anticipate readjustments of a difficult and dangerous type will be helpful in that it tends to avert the panicky fear of another period of unpreparedness for industrial depression. To have it generally known and believed that the government will use all its friendly offices to prevent another industrial catastrophe will have a reassuring effect on those of a doubting mind.

It will be important to have a shelf of public work and projects ready for use, if there is need, available to combat any wide tendency toward general unemployment. The experience with public work and activities during the last eight years will be available and should make it possible to be ready with instant plans for action.[1] Ways and means of financing such a program of activities will also require the most careful preconsideration and specific preparation. But if the full resources of the United States are placed behind the effort and there is general agreement on the desirability of such a program, there is little doubt of the success of the attempt. Such a program will require not only careful planning by governments, federal, state, and local, but will need also the coöperation of private industry in a joint effort to prevent a relapse into deflation and depression.

The relocation both of army personnel and of civilian workers in defense and collateral industries will require the most careful consideration, if the quagmires of unemployment are to be avoided. Employment services must be made more efficient, and if this does not cover the case, additional ways and means must be found. The job and the man must be brought together, even if as a last resort the job has to be made.

The tremendous diversion of ordinary industry into defense production affects profoundly individual industries, individual workers, plant locations, community facilities in various centers of population; and the undoing of this integration and concentration will require equally great attention

[1] See report of NRPB on *Development of Resources and Stabilization of Employment in the U.S.*, 1941.

and equally significant public and private action. The tendency will be doubtless for a helter-skelter return to everything as it was, but in practice such a policy will break down, and may involve the whole country in industrial malaise and even catastrophe. It is easy to give instances of the present-day congestion at numerous points where steel or explosives or ordnance or engines or planes are being produced. If conditions are bad now when these establishments are being set up — and often they are — what will be the conditions when the bugle sounds the retreat from production on a gigantic scale?

Yet all this is not a reason for despair but a challenge to foresight and ability; to judgment and sagacity in broad plans for reconstruction under new conditions. Our national resources and our organizing ability together offer a broad basis upon which it is entirely feasible to make any necessary reconstruction and readjustment in a period of post-emergency transition. In any such crisis, the basic guarantees of democratic participation in the gains of civilization are of the very greatest importance for the community making the readjustments. Employment, security, a fair share in the common good, a feeling that justice is being done to all, a realization that democracy is not a closed book but an open sesame, leading to a finer and richer future than mankind has ever known — these are the un-

derpinning of that morale upon which popular
political association rests in last analysis.

Especially must we plan to bridge over more
successfully than we do now the gulf between
youth and maturity, at all the numerous and difficult points where adjustment is most severe. Youth
as it enters the zone of maturity with all the doubts
and fears of the novitiate should be able to see
stretching out before it the minimum securities as
well as the adventures of human life. Youth should
not look into a future dominated by fear — in an
atmosphere of brutal hazing, so to speak — but look
forward with confident expectation to social justice, liberty, fair participation in the gains of our
common life, in the common good of our time — to
a job, to status, to recognition dependent on ability
and intentions and will, not on the prestige of
others.[1] I am not able at this time to do more than
outline an item on the agenda of democracy, and to
indicate the wide-ranging importance of this problem. Much more serious consideration of this problem is urgent, and indeed is under way. Various
types of approach are of great significance — the
CCC, the NYA, the army training, the summer and
work camps, our vast educational and formal training systems. We may reasonably look forward
toward and diligently plan for important modifications in the transition from the status of youth

[1] Winslow and Davidson, *American Youth* (1940).

to the status of maturity and full participation in the duties and responsibilities and opportunities of American life.

Summarizing, democracy is the ideal form of political association. It provides for the recognition of human dignity, for the expansion of the human personality, for the cultivation of the noblest aspects of human nature — all in the framework of the general welfare and the common good. It provides a principle of fellowship and fraternity, a principle of the consent of the governed, a criterion of reason and justice. Other forms of government are good in so far as they approach the ideals of democratic society. When they attain them fully, they become democratic themselves.

Years ago Jefferson declared that the Constitution of the United States is "not like the ark of the covenant, something too sacred to be touched." Democracy is not merely a form, although forms are involved in its constitution, but a means through which the highest ideals of mankind may be achieved. It is true that the ideals of democracy have not always or even often been fully attained. Its forms have been inadequate to their declared purposes, and its programs have lagged even farther behind from time to time and from place to place. More than once the strength of the democratic appeal to the bulk of mankind has led the temporary holders of authority to identify their own personal or group interests with those of the whole community, and to find in the *status quo* the concluding chapter of democratic development.

But in reality the book is never closed in a democratic association. The course of the general good moves relentlessly forward toward its own appointed ends — sometimes in peaceful channels and again in revolutionary streams and torrents of power. Life, liberty, and the pursuit of happiness flow on in changing demands for human expression, for recognition in constantly novel ways — startling often to those who for the moment are in technical authority but who have forgotten the source of their formal power, the bulk of the community.

It is not undesirable that new demands should be challenged, even sharply challenged; but the onward movement of the democratic mass in a swiftly changing world cannot be denied, or denied with safety. It is with this in mind that I have set out in the preceding pages considerations not only with regard to the rethinking of democracy, and to the streamlining of democracy, but also with regard to the new program of democracy in modern times.

Of all these, the demand for mass participation on a fair basis in the gains of modern civilization is fundamental, and it will not long be denied. Other imperatives are subordinate to this over-all demand for an equitable part of what civilization produces. Those who carry the burdens of the world are not to be denied, for they have seen the light, and are moving toward it in many lands in many ways. Men rise to the challenge of vastly increased productivity of goods and services in a world of chemistry, machinery, biology, management, and organization — in a world scene that presents to us dazzling possibilities of achievement. But they also rise to demand that these new resources shall not be used to brutalize but to elevate life and fill it with finer meaning, to demand just participation in these new and ever increasing riches.

Epilogue

I come now to the end of this agenda of democracy. I have not tried to set down all of the topics that might be included in such a list; or to indicate the precise ways and means of solving and implementing the problems presented. I have even omitted some of my long-time friends such as party systems, urbanism, theories of sovereignty; nationalism, regionalism, the far-flung problems of adjudication. I have passed hastily over many questions of national planning on which I have recently been engaged in the National Resources Planning Board.

I am satisfied if I have made clear the fundamental importance of:

1. Streamlining the structure of democracy in modern form.
2. Recasting the program of democracy, social, economic, cultural, in the light of modern science and discovery.

In conclusion, I sum up the broadest generalizations on the agenda of democracy:

1. The importance of simplifying and energizing the structure of democracy, simplifying it to meet the modern demands for dynamic action, vitalizing the role of legislative direction and supervision on

the one hand and sharpening the tools of administrative management on the other. And drawing together the necessary threads of a jural order of the world.

2. The necessity of a program systematically validating the assumptions of democracy, and specifically guaranteeing that the marvelous gains of our civilization shall be fully realized and made effective in the daily lives of the many as well as the few, not merely in general phrases but in concrete ways.

These broad propositions upon the democratic agenda will aid in the solution of many of our current democratic problems, both external and internal, leading both to the inevitable organization of the jural order of the world and to the internal adjustments thrust upon us by the development of modern science and technology.

Confidence in the ability of government to deal with the common welfare, confidence in a dynamic government responsible to the governed, confidence in the feasibility and desirability of diffusing fairly among the community the gains of modern civilization — these are guides in dealing with many of the puzzling questions of the democratic political society.

Some of the points of a program based upon such considerations have been indicated in the preceding chapters of this volume, but necessarily only the broadest outlines could be given within the compass of this general sketch. Nor do I have access to all the answers, even if there were ample space for elaboration. Many of the questions raised will require elaborate inquiry, careful analysis, and careful and persistent implementation over a considerable period of time. And in any case the means of democracy will always be subject to readjustment to democracy's ends, with changing social circumstances. One of the points I have most strongly emphasized, indeed, is the serious danger of confusing means and forms with ends, and of defending the *status quo* instead of the genuine development of democratic principles.

Democracy is the best form of government yet devised by the brain of man — the ideal form of political association — most perfectly realized under ideal conditions. This is not to say that other and competing forms do not have an historical justification in various periods of political development. "A slave people," said Montesquieu, "can have nothing but their chains." Semi-slave and undeveloped peoples of varying types are scattered along the ways of time. Many historic democracies were only partly democratic. Persuasion and reason are the ideal forms of social adjustment, but violence, a lower form of organization, is widespread over broad ranges of political behavior. Nevertheless, the goal we contemplate, the ideal toward which we work, is that of fraternal association in which the consent of the governed is basic, and peace is a means of attaining the highest form of life within a society, or between societies.

The revolutionary quality of democracy may make it fearful to some, but this restless spirit arises not merely from desire for change but also from capacity for change and adjustment, without prejudice to the principle upon which the system rests. Free society is flexible society. If it contains within itself the seeds of destruction, it also contains the renewing and reconstructing power of human intelligence, the human fraternal spirit. The regenerating democratic qualities are stronger in last analysis than the dark powers of fear, hate, cruelty, ignorance. Intelligence and idealism are not weak, but strong and expansive, creative in the real sense of the term.

On the program of democracy is the forward and upward look, the vision of what man might attain by human invention and adjustment in the modern world — the standards of living, the intellectual advantages, the sense of security, the cultural and spiritual gains, the flowering of personalities too often crushed down in the mad rush, the fraternal sense of participation in a world from which the many have been thrust out or forgotten on its outer fringes.

If all this seems revolutionary or even fantastic,

we may reply that it may be revolutionary but it is not fabulous or fantastic. Within the framework of our resources, democratic ideals and institutions may be made to flower now.

We stand at the gates of an age of plenty, key in hand, fumbling at the lock. Before us lies, not some unrealistic Utopia, but a common-sense world of struggle in which human and material resources have been organized for the joint purpose of (1) maximum productivity and (2) fair diffusion of the resulting gains.

Never were so many restless and discontented peoples under so many flags and so many leaders in so many scattered lands seeking for a sign and a symbol of the good life in which their cherished and legitimate aspirations might be realized. In their confusion they often turn upon each other. But if they identify democracy with its true spirit and aims rather than its imperfections and aberrations, they will find that fraternalism, sharing the gains of civilization, world security arising from a world order, the intelligent and full development of human resources, the guaranties of liberty and justice arising from the participation of the community in the determination of the common good, provide the formula they seek.

At the end of any cycle of despots, dictators, autocrats, juggling with popular morale, professing popular welfare, comes the slow return of power back to the community from whom power ultimately arises. The revolt against democracy thus swings back again to democracy, itself the most revolutionary force in human society, but both revolutionary and developmental, and rational rather than violent in its modes of action.

The days of little-restricted *laissez-faire*, the days when government was looked upon as a necessary evil — these have gone for a long time, perhaps forever, although in the mutations of time one never knows what forms may recur. In their place have come discovery, invention, management — a technological world in which pestilence, famine, and warfare are unwelcome intruders whatever their momentary triumphs, a world in which organization and power have new meanings implicit in the nature of the new world in which they come. Nondemocratic states have seen some of the evils of our day, but they have not understood the gains of our time, nor do they understand the broad directives of the future, leading to paths of peace, to coöperation, fraternity, prosperity based upon the world's expanded productivity.

It may be said, you are demanding not merely a form of political association but a change in unchangeable human nature itself. Perhaps this is indeed the point at which the issue should really be joined. But if so, then both science and the angels are on the side of those who look forward to far-reaching betterments, not in human nature but in its organization and its possibilities of personal development through enriched forms of association. Pestilence, war, famine, flood, and fire — fear, want, life that is "nasty, poor, brutish and short," mental and physical distress and torture — these are not decreed by nature but are within our own power to command and control. The stream of life forces, the waters of life, are not our grim foes dragging us down to inexorable doom; they are ourselves for weal as well as woe. The human spirit through science, reason, faith, may bring light and life and healing on its wings, if we so will.

We cannot trace precisely the blueprints of emerging forms of human association, but we have drawn from human reason and experience the outlines, blurred and marred though they may be, of a fraternal order of mankind in which the basic assumptions of democracy provide the framework of justice, liberty, order, welfare, peace.

INDEX

INDEX

VILLANOVA COLLEGE LIBRARY

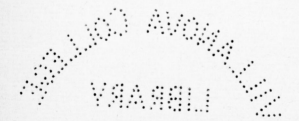

F...TY ...RARY

Date Due